THE PARABLES

THE PARABLES

Daniel R. Seagren

 Tyndale House
Publishers, Inc.
Wheaton, Illinois

Dedicated to the memory

of my mother

Selma Augusta Hill Seagren

Library of Congress Catalog Card
Number 77-083570
ISBN 0-8423-4797-6
Copyright © 1978 by Tyndale House Publishers,
Inc., Wheaton, Illinois. All rights reserved.
First printing, April 1978.
Printed in the United States of America.

CONTENTS

Index of Parables Studied

PREFACE

There are many books already written about the parables of Jesus. Why another?

Many of these are excellent—some are even classics. There are the familiar names of Bruce, Cadoux, and Dodd, as well as Hunter, Jeremias, and Thielicke.

Herbert Lockyer ambitiously penned *All the Parables of the Bible*, and Charles E. Carlston examined the editing of Matthew, Mark, and Luke in his *The Parables of the Triple Tradition*. And why not?

It *is* important to know something about all of the parables, and it does make a difference if Matthew placed a parable in Chapter 13 or Chapter 24 (with our apologies to Matthew, who didn't use chapters and verses).

Although scholarship will not be ignored, the major thrust of this study is aimed at those who live and

work on Main Street rather than the theologians and
scholars who reside in ivory towers. Consequently,
deliberate efforts will be made to avoid dropping names
or embellishing the pages with cumbersome footnotes.

I would suggest you read the appropriate passage
carefully before reading my discussion of it. There will
be a deliberate attempt to "think Palestinian." These
parables were told (and then written) in an atmosphere
dissimilar to the twentieth century. Bridging ancient
cultures with contemporary society is not easily done,
but must be done if we are to have full understanding.

Some have tried too hard, others not at all.

This study will attempt to bring our own culture into
a meaningful relationship with the culture of the
past without completely abandoning either. Simply put,
this means that there will be a few compromises. Or
possibly even taking some liberties in expanding the
parable without, hopefully, changing its nature.

There will also be a deliberate attempt to "think
parabolically." There are sometimes great individual
differences in the definition of the word "parable." In fact,
we are not totally certain what Jesus or the authors of
the Gospels meant by the term. Not with absolute
precision.

Therefore, a couple of important things must be done.

The first will be to more or less define what we mean by
"parable," then apply this to Matthew, Mark, and Luke
as best we can. This definition, to be developed in the
Introduction, will be a working definition, flexible
enough to be able to twist and turn throughout the pages
which follow.

And then there will be an attempt to "think
provincially."

To many, "provincial" suggests narrow, backward
country thinking. It can indeed be a rather caustic label.
However, there are times and places where it is to be
desired.

Recently a close friend, a rabbi, lamented the fact that
so many of his colleagues are so thoroughly secular.

Quietly, but with regrets, I acknowledged that this is true among clergymen as well. Our sorrow brought us even closer. Too many rabbis and priests, ministers and theologians consider the Good News (Old or New) to be little more than ragged bits of nostalgia. A new generation needs a new gospel. Or does it?

The parables serve as a check and balance system on the gospel. Not only are they masterpieces of ancient literature, they sit in judgment of the Good News.

If we disregard the Man from Galilee, the parables quickly remind us of who he was and what he had in mind.

If we quibble over the exact words of the itinerant preacher from Nazareth, the parables forcibly drive home his message.

If we had nothing except the parables of Jesus, Christendom would not be totally impoverished. To the contrary, because we have the' parables, we cannot stray too far from the beaten path Jesus trod. As we study the parables, we study Christianity. A provincial Christianity.

Not provincial in the sense of being countrified in speech or manners—or even narrow-minded. But rather, provincial in the sense of getting deeply involved in the authority and dialect of a knowledge which is limited in perspective. The parables disallow us from creating an all-things-to-all-men Christianity.

One more thing.

The parables are provincial, but they are also the opposite. They are universal.

The word "Christian," when first used, was probably a derogatory nickname given to the early believers. However, Christendom and Christianity, as expressions, were foreign to the Gospel writers. They used another expression: the Kingdom of God (or the Kingdom of Heaven).

Everyone then had a general understanding of the meaning of kingdom and consequently was able to readily grasp the concept of the Kingdom of God.

Today, in a practical sense, we can substitute the idea of Christendom or Christianity for the kingdom concept. But as we do so, we must retain a double meaning of the word "kingdom."

In its broadest sense, kingdom can mean the world at large as influenced, directly or indirectly, by a sovereignty. In other words, the Kingdom of God's jurisdiction reaches beyond the world of its constituents, just as the authority and effects of Christianity extend beyond the community of believers.

But in the narrower sense, a kingdom is limited to its subjects. Again, this is true of Christianity as seen in the Church, the Body of Christ.

To do justice to the nature and scope of the Kingdom of God (and the concept of Christendom), we must keep in mind both dimensions: the broad and the narrow. In this way we shall look at the parables: provincial, yet universal; temporal, but eternal.

INTRODUCTION:
A PARABLE IS...

There is little agreement on exactly what a parable is.

This is readily seen when dipping into parabolic literature. The parable has been defined simply as "an earthly story with a heavenly meaning." This definition is probably more profound than it first appears. However, not all parables are *earthly* stories (for example, Lazarus and the rich man in the two compartments of a place for the dead). And though the meaning of parables is in a sense *heavenly*, they have to do not only with the afterlife but with the way we live here and now.

The parable has also been defined as "a short story with a hidden or spiritual meaning." This definition is not nearly as perceptive. Nor is this one: "a simple story illustrating a religious or moral lesson." Dictionaries do not tell it all, nor can they. We must probe deeper.

Others put it this way: "A parable is a verbal stick of dynamite with an indiscriminate fuse" (one never knows when it will explode). And still another definition: "A parable is a good yarn in which the unknown is explained by the known."

We could continue, but this will illustrate the point. Just when we think we have a good definition, it fades. In fact, it might well be impossible to find a satisfactory definition, one that fits all parables. It might help to examine what a parable is not, and then come back to a working definition of the biblical parable.

To begin with, a parable is not a fable. There are some marvelous fables in literature, especially those of Aesop. In a fable, a deeper meaning is suggested in a fictional story which is often centered around animal characters or legendary personalities. Normally we think of fables as having a moral, but rarely does a fable illuminate a religious or spiritual truth. In this sense, although similar in style, the two differ significantly in content. A fable can be timeless but not eternal. It could be ingenious but not infallible.

Parables defy exhaustion; the more we study them, the more we learn. We continually discover new insights and deeper meanings. Fables are charming and disarming, and some are even enchantingly subtle. They climb the stairway to the stars, but never quite reach them. The parable continues where the fable ends. The parable also reaches for the stars but continues on into eternity.

In this sense, a parable is an earthly story with a heavenly meaning, but a fable is a heavenly (charming) story with an earthly meaning. Though similar, they are worlds apart.

If parables and fables are easily confused—and they are—how about parables and allegories?

In plain terms, an allegory is a story—simple or complex—in which many if not all of the details have a symbolic (or deeper) meaning. Allegories can be delightful, earthy, fable-type stories, and they can be mysteriously abstract.

A Parable Is . . .

Allegories are often used to teach or explain, and sometimes are deliberately designed to encourage, or even force, a person into probing more deeply into a subject.

Not all allegories, however, are abstract, and many are second-cousin to the parable. In fact, some parables are what we could call *allegorical parables* and some allegories could be termed *parabolic allegories*.

Confusing, isn't it? This is why it is almost impossible not only to define parables but to categorize them. Consider the parable of the good Samaritan. Certain scholars have called this an allegory and have assigned symbolic meanings to each element of the story: the road, the bandits, victim, priest, Levite, Samaritan, donkey, inn, innkeeper, etc. Others claim that it is strictly a parable and the participants must not be allegorized. As we shall see later, this is probably an allegorical parable (rather than a parabolic allegory) with strong restraints necessary on the imaginative handling of the parable.

To further complicate the subject, parables are also sometimes confused with analogies. In an analogy, the unknown is usually compared to the known, the difficult with the more obvious, in an attempt to clarify or simplify —or to make visible that which is invisible or hidden.

For instance, we could say that life is like a roller coaster: it has its ups and downs with some sharp curves here and there. In many ways—but not all—we could say that life is analogous to a roller coaster.

Jesus said that the Kingdom of God is like a mustard seed. He also said, "Blessed are the meek, for they shall inherit the earth." Although they both say somewhat the same thing, the analogy gives a much more vivid picture.

Analogies, the comparison of things usually unlike but with certain related similarities, can be dangerous. There is the temptation to compare all of the dimensions rather than the ones intended. We can do parables, allegories, and analogies considerable damage by either pushing them too far or not far enough, or by not carefully distinguishing between them. A parable can be created in the form of an allegory or an analogy, but basically remains what it was intended to be: a parable.

Consequently, a parable could be considered by certain scholars to be a pure parable but others would argue for a blend, let's say of eighty percent metaphor and twenty percent parable. Another could be fifty percent parable, thirty percent analogy, and twenty percent allegory. As you can see, this method of reckoning could easily destroy the character as well as the message of the parable.

Perhaps it would be wise to consider some of the other figures of speech—particularly those closely related to the parable—and define them in a practical manner. This definition style is deliberately (and dangerously) sketchy, but it will illustrate the complexity of defining parables since so many of the parables are strengthened by the various figures of speech. These definitions will also serve as reference points for the subsequent pages.

Allegory—a story, poem, or word-picture in which a spiritual or poetic meaning is conveyed symbolically.

Analogy—a comparison of two unlike things which share certain similarities.

Anecdote—an account of a happening which is told to make or illustrate a point or to evoke a response (humor, pathos, anger, rapport, etc.).

Fable—an imaginative story designed to convey a moral, often employing animals or objects as communicating characters.

Idiom—a mode of expression whereby the real meaning is not understood by a normal understanding of the words (e.g., shoot the breeze).

Illustration—a story or an example used to clarify, enrich, reinforce, or possibly help prove a certain idea or pattern of thought.

Metaphor—a word or a phrase used to convey another meaning (e.g., a copper sky, a burning temper, etc.).

Myth—a legendary or traditional attempt to explain or account for events in nature, history, and religion, particularly as they relate to the supernatural.

A Parable Is . . .

Narrative—a series of connected details used in story-telling, poetry, and drama to describe or explain.

Proverb—a short local or universal saying which has stood the test of time and contains special truth or wisdom.

Rhetorical question—a question which is raised in order to evoke a response without expecting or receiving an answer.

Riddle—a puzzling question, statement, or problem which requires an answer or a solution.

Simile—a figure of speech in which two essentially unlike things are compared (such as smart as a whip, cheeks like roses, etc.).

Story—a relating of an event (or a series of events), fictional or true, usually in a detailed manner.

Ironically, parables contain elements of all these figures of speech. This not only makes them unique but exciting. We can begin to recognize the wonders of the parable, not only by examining those in Scripture, but by trying to create parables of our own (and soon discovering how difficult they are to compose). It is little wonder that the apostles were content to live with the parables of Jesus rather than invent their own. Parables, as a literary device, are not unique; but among parables, those of Jesus are.

Now let's attempt to develop a working definition of the word "parable."

The word has suffered from two extremes. One viewpoint has sought for a deeper meaning in the parables than they warrant. It is easy (but dangerous) to read more into a parable than Jesus intended. One example of this is found among scholars who over-allegorize the parables.

The other extreme rejects any allegorical understanding, seeking only for the one, singular, general truth Jesus was trying to convey.

The well-loved story of the prodigal son can illustrate the tendency to get too much out of a parable.

Tertullian assigned specific roles to each part of the

story. The elder son is the Jew, and the younger (prodigal) son represents the Christian. The employer in the far country is the devil. The robe symbolizes the sonship which Adam lost, and the ring is the sign and seal of baptism. The celebration feast is the Lord's Supper, and the fatted calf represents Christ who was slain for us. It's easy to see that this kind of interpretation can lead to misleading *eisegesis*.

However, to oversimplify a parable in order to make it a "pure parable" (without allegorical or metaphorical meaning) presents another kind of danger. A pure parable is one which makes a single, dominant point—no more and no less. An example of this might be to say that the parable of the prodigal son has one message: delinquent behavior leads to grief.

Now, while the parable does teach that, that's not all it teaches—and interpretations such as this are regrettable. To retitle the parable "The Waiting Father" is better exegesis, although it too is only part of the message. The fact is that the parables are complex stories, and we must continually resist the temptation to interpret them unwisely by making them say too much or too little.

At the time of Christ, parables and fables were popular figures of speech. The Eastern mind had a flair for the imaginative use of speech as against a more intellectual and logical mode of expression. The listeners often failed to grasp the subtle and deeper meanings of the parables of Jesus, but not because they were unaccustomed to such communications. Jesus took an ancient and revered style of speech and created his own ingenious and unequaled style.

In reading the sayings of Jesus, we can hardly claim that he was unimaginative. His parables ranged all the way from simple, pithy sayings such as "How can the blind lead the blind?" to the detailed, masterly story of the good Samaritan. If we fill in the details of a blind man leading another blind man, we have a parable just as full of meaning as his poignant story of the good neighbor.

But what is a parable?

A Parable Is . . .

The Greek word for parable in the New Testament is a
compound word, *parabolē*: *para* (a preposition meaning
near, beside, with, in, etc.) and *ballō* (to throw, rather
vigorously). Putting these two words together we come up
with something like this: "to throw something with force
at someone." This evolves, then, to mean "placing
something alongside another," which evolves even more
into "something which resembles or has a likeness for the
purpose of comparison."

Therefore, a parable is a *picturesque form of speech
created to make an impact upon the listener.* And that is
exactly what the parables did—and what they are still
doing. Perhaps the term refers not so much to the literary
form of the parable as to its intent or effect.

This actually implies that there is no firmly fixed
definition possible for the expression *parable*. Parables
come in all sizes and shapes, in words and deeds, as
similes, metaphors, allegories, fables, illustrations,
stories, anecdotes, analogies, riddles, and proverbs
(among other figures of speech), and possibly even in
scratches in the sand.

Therefore, we must do the impossible: we must come
up with a working definition of the term *parable*.

Here it is—*Parable*: an ingenious figure of speech,
usually a short story of everyday life, which teaches a
singular spiritual truth, as well as suggesting subordinate
truths.

KINGDOM PARABLES

CHAPTER ONE
THE ABSENTEE LANDLORD
Matthew 21:33-46
Mark 12:1-12
Luke 20:9-19

Should the parables be studied chronologically?

Sounds good, but it's an impossibility. No one can be absolutely certain when or where Jesus spoke the parables —or (sometimes) exactly to whom.

In this case, however, Matthew, Mark, and Luke are pretty well agreed that it is one of the last parables of Jesus. The reason why we want to begin with it is because it provides such a masterful panorama of the Good News.

Jesus had just been acclaimed (unofficially) King of the Jews as he was royally ushered into Jerusalem. Men and women, boys and girls showered the roadway with palms. But it was a strange ride. Kings normally entered capital cities mounted on a powerful stallion or riding ceremoniously in a royal chariot. But not Jesus. He rode a donkey.

His kingship began in a mysterious humility, but soon
took on other overtones. Before many hours had lapsed,
Jesus was paralyzing the treacherous religious leadership
with his devastating questions and piercing parables—
and his audacious acts.

"Who gave you the authority to do these things?"
they barked.

Jesus made a deal with them. "If you'll answer my
question, I'll answer yours. Was John's baptism from
heaven or from men?"

Putting their heads together, his adversaries quickly
realized they were trapped. If John had been a servant of
God, then why hadn't they believed him? And if they said
John wasn't a prophet, the crowd would turn against
them. They could only answer they didn't know.

Jesus kept his word and refused to answer their
question. Jesus won this round. In fact, he won all the
rounds. They couldn't handle his parables either. (See
Mark 11:27-33.)

It was at this point that Jesus threw this parable at
them. Whether he was only addressing the religious
opposition, we do not know. Presumably he spoke these
words for his disciples as well. Perhaps more so. In either
case, it was normal procedure for the Sanhedrin to
publicly test any religious leader; but it was hardly
normal for the sophisticated Sanhedrin to be humiliated
by a country rabbi.

The quip should be amended (perhaps it has been) to
be a bit more realistic: if you can't lick 'em, join 'em or
eliminate 'em. The Sanhedrin chose the latter.

Jesus set the wheels of his fate into motion by driving
the scandalous moneychangers out of the temple (a
parable in pantomime) and by clobbering his critics with
a coin (Mark 11:15-18; 12:13-17).

And to add—as we say—insult to injury, Jesus told the
story about a man who planted a vineyard and sublet it
to sharecroppers. Having agreed on terms, he took off on a
long journey while the sharecroppers worked the
vineyard.

The Absentee Landlord

When the time arrived to settle accounts, the owner sent one of his business associates to collect his share of the crop. The opportunistic sharecroppers, however, beat this associate and sent him back empty-handed. The owner sent another associate to collect the debt, and he too was mistreated. He sent another whom they killed and several others who were shamefully mistreated. (The Gospel accounts differ in number, but the idea remains the same.)

Finally, the patient owner reasoned to himself, "I'll send my son. Surely they will respect him." They didn't. When the son arrived, the wicked and foolish sharecroppers gloated, "This is the heir. If we kill him, the vineyard will be ours." They killed the son and cast his body out of the vineyard.

At this point, Jesus paused and asked his jittery audience a question—"What will the owner do now?"

The scribes and Pharisees knew exactly what the owner would do. He would do what they would do. He would come personally, destroy the wicked sharecroppers, and sublet the vineyard to those worthy of it.

Jesus made no direct comment on their answer. Instead, he dug up an obscure phrase out of their Psalm Book (118:22)—the one about the stone which was rejected by the builders but later became the honored cornerstone. Luke includes another phrase (20:18) which was probably taken from one of the Prophets. It candidly states that whoever trips over that stone will be broken to bits; but if the stone falls on anyone, it will crush him into dust (see Isaiah 8:14, 15).

By now the scribes and Pharisees were seething with anger and frustration, because if they touched Jesus the people would turn against them. They waited for a more opportune moment.

Matthew tells us that Jesus recognized the accuracy of their answer, but also drove this message deep into their hardening conscience: "Listen, the Kingdom of God shall be taken away from you and given to another nation." Then the Pharisees knew that he was talking about them.

No wonder they wanted him out of the way.

Jesus was talking autobiographically; but more than that, he was giving a nutshell history of God's dealings with his people. Jesus does not interpret the entire parable, but he does explain part of it. From this explanation we know that the parable is in part allegorical. This brings us to the intricate task of unveiling the allegory without distorting the parable.

We could attempt to read into the various servants (associates) individual names, but this would be suicidal to the parable. It is possible, however, to suggest that they represent various key personalities in the owner's relationship to the vineyard. But we are getting ahead of our story.

During early New Testament times, much of the country was owned by absentee landlords. The disciples as well as the Sanhedrin understood the tension and bitterness this caused. Jesus was dealing with a sensitive issue, one that was very much alive. The Hebrew nation had been splintered and destroyed as a people, taken into captivity, and a remnant returned to their homeland little more than serfs.

The Jewish people were at the mercy of their rulers and absentee landlords. At best, they were sharecroppers. Therefore, it was not uncommon for the local people to barter for the best possible deal with an absentee landlord, who might or might not be reasonable.

There was also a law in the land which entitled sharecroppers to stake a claim on the land they had been working. If and when a landowner died and left no heir, the sharecroppers could inherit the land, providing no other legal provision had already been made. Many ill-conceived plots had been laid down through the years in this struggle for the land.

What does all this mean, and what does it have to do with Christ's gospel?

Going back into the earliest history of mankind—to the refugees outside Eden—we see that God had a plan. The Good News is not an accident.

The Absentee Landlord

Originally parents were to pass on the fruits of their knowledge and experience. Adam and Eve, badly burned by curiosity and compromise, disobedience and defiance, had the scars to show Cain and Abel. How seriously they took their parenting we cannot say, but we do know that a tragedy occurred and their family fell apart.

Before long, the workable (theoretically) parent-child transmission failed, and others were entrusted with additional responsibility. Although they were to supplement the parental task, often they carried the full burden. An entire sequence of leaders—patriarchs, judges, prophets, priests, and kings—entered and exited from the scene with an enormous display of altars, laws, tabernacles, Temples, and synagogues.

Finally, God sent his own Son to pull it all together. The sacrificial system was fulfilled and the law enriched, the Scriptures slowly fell into place, kings were replaced by the King of kings, and the Temple in Jerusalem gave way to the temple of the Holy Spirit, the body of the Christian believer.

Since Jesus' own received him not, the burden passed on to those who would. It has been through them—faulty as they are—that the Good News has gone forth during these centuries.

Now the parable is beginning to take shape.

The vineyard represents a small nation of people entrusted with a given task. God had entrusted the responsibility to the sharecroppers, repeatedly sending messengers, many of whom were shamefully treated. Even his Son was rejected. So the responsibility was taken from them and shifted to others.

It is imperative, however, that we regard this as a parable. It is not an allegory. We simply cannot assign symbolical meanings to each detail without artificially and systematically destroying the message of the parable.

The disciples would soon be witnessing the death of their beloved country rabbi. Although Jesus had been preparing them for this (and God had been doing the same through the ages), the realization of what was happening quickly terrorized the disciples and scattered them among the hills.

Jesus knew this was going to happen. That's why he wanted his disciples, as well as the whole Sanhedrin, to see the whole panorama of his coming, to know that he was the Son and God was the owner who not only owns a vineyard but the cattle on a thousand hills. He wanted his disciples to know that he was the stone which would be rejected, yet would emerge as the chief cornerstone of a new and living church. He wanted them to know that he would die an ignoble death, and that his Father would *not* crush his enemies in a fit of anger.

It was the scribes and Pharisees who said that the owner should kill the malicious sharecroppers and give the vineyard away to more deserving tenants, not Jesus. Jesus, like his Father, was not out for blood. Just the same, Jesus' words would lead to bloodshed as the Pharisees realized that Jesus had seen through their hypocrisy and sham. But it was this same blood which was spilled for them, although they knew it not.

They thought they had the final word when they later protested Pilate's inscription: JESUS OF NAZARETH—KING OF THE JEWS. As they watched Jesus take his final breath, little did they realize how wrong Pilate really was. The inscription should have read: JESUS OF NAZARETH—KING OF KINGS. But that isn't what the Sanhedrin had in mind. They thought he shouldn't claim any royalty at all.

Jesus, in a simple little story, wrapped up the history of mankind. He revealed God's plan for the Good News, a plan that was created before the foundations of the earth were laid, not as an afterthought.

God knew fully well that his creation, man, would rebel sooner or later, and that man would need a plan of redemption. Remember the parable—God allowed the farmers to choose between commitment or rebellion. He removed himself from the scene, but not entirely. God abandoned us to ourselves and our folly, but he didn't abandon us totally (more about this in the parable of the prodigal son).

Now that we have seen that the Good News is just that— good news—we should be able to better understand what the scribes and Pharisees feared so much. They knew he was for real and that if they didn't stop him quickly, they might not be able to stop him at all. (And, of course, they weren't.)

How little they really understood.

And how little the disciples understood—at the time.

CHAPTER TWO
SMUG SECURITY
AND CREATIVE RISK
Matthew 25:14-30
Luke 19:12-27

Here are two incongruent parables.

Some have tried to make these two parables brothers, or even identical twins. It is impossible, or at least impractical. (Actually, they're more like second cousins.)

Some have tried to show that one is the offspring of an earlier story of Jesus, while others say they are not even distantly related. Both opinions are probably inexact as we shall discover.

Some will argue that Luke probably picked up a hand-me-down version, while Matthew heard the original parable. Consequently, they argue, the Matthew account is more precise. But we have no evidence that the physician was too far removed to be a valid witness, or that Matthew was a better listener, although it is quite likely that Matthew heard many of the parables firsthand while Luke heard the secondhand version. Here is a good place to say a kind word about oral tradition.

As practiced at that time in the Eastern world, oral tradition had developed into a highly skilled technique. When something important was to be preserved, it was memorized with a precision few of us can appreciate. In fact, oral traditions can be far more faithful—and often are—than written traditions. Sleepy, bored scribes have probably misspelled and omitted more words (and even sentences) than we may ever know. We need not worry about a parable being told many times. It was undoubtedly told exactly the way it was heard the first time.

We shall attempt to probe into each parable separately —because they are different parables—but we will also show that they are companion parables. In a sense, they are two sides of the same coin (which is not a bad figure of speech since both use money to illustrate a point).

Normally considered judgment parables, there is good reason to consider these parables early in our study.

If the Christian life were all options and no commands, it would make little or no difference how we accepted our responsibilities.

We could with clear conscience accept our salvation without working it out with fear and trembling.

We wouldn't have to sow seed.

We wouldn't have to leave the ninety and nine.

We wouldn't have to sell all that we have to buy a field with the hidden treasure buried in it.

We wouldn't have to worry about extending the Kingdom of God or growing in righteousness.

With these thoughts, we can now plunge into the area of Christian responsibility. That is what these parables are about.

THE PARABLE OF THE TALENTS

Matthew's account gives what has been known as the parable of the talents (KJV), an unfortunate juxtaposition of words.

Smug Security and Creative Risk

The biblical word translated "talent" refers to a certain weight of silver or gold or whatever; i.e., it is a monetary term. In this particular time, a talent was a considerable sum, especially for a person of average income.

For practical purposes, rather than bicker about the exact worth, let's use the figure of $1,000 per talent. This meant that one person received $5,000, the others $2,000 and $1,000 respectively—each according to his ability to handle the money effectively and appropriately. Each of the three was to invest the money for his master (employer) while he was gone.

This was not a gift to these men. It was capital to be invested in order to earn more money for the master.

Unfortunately, we automatically equate talents (money) with talents (skills or abilities). This is not quite what the parable is saying.

If we talk of five-talent, two-talent, and one-talent people, we are realistic but not in step with the parable. The talent as used here represents the responsibility our Master gives each of us in the light of our capabilities and opportunities. In other words, the Lord does not place a heavier burden on our shoulders than we can bear, but he does give us a task and expects us to get on with it.

As believers, we all have different opportunities and capacities, different dispositions and personalities. Our situations are not identical; they vary constantly.

The principal character in this story knew his servants —their temperaments, physical strength, academic and business acumen, family obligations, personal skills, and mental attitude. With all these in mind, the wise entrepreneur (or whatever he was) called the three men to him and gave each of them a responsibility.

It is even possible that he did this privately, so that each of the men did not know the capital sums involved. This is conjecture, but a defendable one. No believer knows what another's responsibility is. Not totally or precisely anyway.

Therefore, each investor acted accordingly. He did his own thing in his own way. And when it came time for accounting, each was responsible—not to the other servants—but to the boss.

The boss (a term we all understand) judged each man, not by how much he had earned, but because he tried or didn't try. Two of the men doubled their capital, but there is no implication that with a little more effort they could have tripled the money. The whole story hinges on the fact that the boss was happy with their efforts because they fulfilled their obligation according to their ability to do so. They were trustworthy and faithful, and so commended accordingly.

Too often we read into this parable that those with the most talent get the most reward. Or even worse, those with no talent get no reward.

The third investor was severely rebuked. Why? Simply because he earned no money for his employer? No, the parable doesn't say this. In fact, it is quite possible that he would have been commended even if he had lost some, or even all, of the money, providing he had at least sincerely tried.

The heart of the parable is not that we must be successful, but that we must be faithful.

It is possible that we will work diligently for years as Christians and have little or perhaps nothing to show for it. Some missionaries have worked for years—even decades—with no visible results. But subsequent missionaries have reaped a bountiful harvest. The Lord made it clear as he told this parable that there will be a multitude of complicating factors entered into the reckoning. When we show him the ledger of our investments, he may nod in agreement or shake his head in amazement, but he will evaluate it in the light of our abilities and opportunities. It is only when we show him a blank ledger that he will throw the book at us.

The servant who received the five talents ($5,000) had turned it into $10,000, but the one who buried the $1,000 for safekeeping had it taken away from him and given to the one with $10,000. This isn't fair, say many. And it isn't, in a way.

Smug Security
and Creative Risk

We must remember that there is not the slightest suggestion in the parable that these servants were given this money as a gift. They were given the original sum as capital to invest, and the obvious interpretation is that they were also given the second figure, not to keep, but to invest.

It must be presumed that all the while they were investing the money, they received their salary as servants (room and board and spending money at least). This was their job. They didn't actually have an option, even though the third servant thought he did.

A word about him seems to be in order at this point.

He seems to be a complex personality. He was evidently caustic in his remarks to the boss. He recognized the power and prestige of his master, who made money even without touching it (by entrusting funds to faithful employees—and possibly other means).

Realizing his employer was very demanding, the third servant decided to wrap the money (probably coins) in a cloth napkin. This may sound a bit strange until we realize it was a customary way of preserving cash. However, there was a safer way: to bury it in the ground.

Had he only kept the money wrapped in a cloth, he would have been liable for its theft or mysterious disappearance. By burying it, he invoked a law of the land which made him not liable for its loss. Therefore, he protected both his master and himself.

From this it can be determined that he was not totally an irresponsible person. He was safety-minded and showed concern for his own protection. He did not want to accept responsibility for handling the money because he might make an unwise or even foolish investment. It would be, he seemed to reason, wiser to preserve the entire $1,000 than to lose all or a portion of it (or even to merely increase it slightly). Besides, to his credit, he could have squandered all or part of it on himself— but he didn't.

What was wrong? Was he lazy or indifferent? Timorous or afraid? Whatever the reason, he came up with a lame excuse and the employer didn't buy it. At least, said the boss, you could have put the money into a bank where it would have earned interest.

Throughout all of this, it is obvious that the third servant wasn't as naive as it might appear. Consequently, his fate seems somewhat harsh although it is based upon his deliberate faithlessness, not his lack of skill.

There is a double jeopardy here, as there usually is.

Not only was he punished, but an added responsibility was added to the one who already was carrying a heavy burden. What appears to be a reward is also added responsibility. Because the task was too important to neglect, what one will not do, someone else must do.

THE PARABLE OF THE POUNDS

As in the previous parable, this story was told to the disciples shortly before the crucifixion, at the time when Jesus was gradually turning the responsibilities of the Kingdom of God over to them.

It, too, deals with the subject of responsibility, although it handles it in a different manner.

In this story a nobleman, a man with power and probably wealth, was going to a distant country where he was to be crowned king. During his absence, he presumably had several missions he wanted accomplished at home.

One of these was to keep his capital working for him. Considering that the pound (KJV) is a rather small sum of money compared to the talent, the stress is not as much on the amount. For practical purposes, let's say that a pound is worth $200 (rather than quibble about exact figures).

It also seems likely that the nobleman was interested in keeping his ten men busy while he was gone. This is of course only implied, but certainly not out of the question. We have a saying that "when the cat is away, the mice play." The Swedes say that "when the cat is away, the rats dance on the table." Either way, idleness—whether in an employee or a disciple—breeds mischief.

Then again, it might be argued that the nobleman wanted to prove the worth of his men. What they did with the money would tell him considerable.

As in the parable of the talents, we have an accounting of three servants. We do not know what the other seven did, although we can conjecture. At any rate, the message is much more clearly seen with only three responses.

Again, the two parables are similar but different. The nobleman called ten servants and gave them ten pounds ($2,000). This is considerably less than the three servants in the other parable who received $1,000, $2,000 and $5,000 respectively.

Earlier we suggested that each servant perhaps received the capital (talents) privately since each amount was different. Here, however, the context seems to indicate that the nobleman called ten of his servants together and gave them ten pounds collectively (see Luke 19:13, KJV). It is not until the period of accounting that the servants told the master that they had taken their one pound and turned it into ten and five and kept it safely in a napkin.

The assumption, which again is conjecture, is that the servants, after receiving the ten pounds, decided to divide it evenly. If this is the case, and we will assume that it is, it makes a considerable difference between the two parables and their ultimate meaning.

In the first parable, we think in terms of individual responsibility, dependent upon the person's ability to handle the investment. In this parable, we think of collective responsibility whereby a group of servants were given a task.

In the former, the servant had no choice in the capital he received. In the latter, the servants decided themselves how to assign the capital (with the three each stating what they had done with their original $200).

This dual responsibility makes sense. We each have a job to do in the Kingdom which is strictly our own. This responsibility is important—and we dare not ignore it.

These responsibilities vary from person to person and are given, not by others, but by the Lord himself.

On the other hand, we are in this thing together. There are tasks to be done, and we can divvy them up as we decide. Likening this, for instance, to a congregation, we could say that the Body of Christ has a collective task in a community, a task shared by all its members.

Even so, some will be far more productive than others, for many reasons. If a congregation of 100 members could divide its responsibility into 100 equal shares (which of course it cannot), it would be inevitable that some would run with the task, others would walk, and some would lie down.

Putting the two parables side by side suggests that perhaps the ten servants were not wisest in dividing the original ten pounds evenly. What if the servant who increased his share tenfold had received half of the pounds as his capital to work with? He could then have turned the five into fifty. But now we are digressing too far.

Perhaps, however, we could say that there are tasks which ought to be assigned to groups rather than individuals, and that there is such a thing as collective as well as individual responsibility. Could it be that the nobleman intended the ten servants to work as a unit but they divided (splintered) the task into equal shares with rather uneven results? Could it be that the first servant who piloted his pound into ten could have encouraged servant number three, keeping him from merely protecting his share?

We must remember that Jesus was preparing his disciples for their role as members of a fledgling community which he called the Kingdom of God, knowing that they would not only work together as a team but also be scattered to the wind where they would work individually until they could rebuild another unit.

Either way, we as believers have both individual and collective responsibilities which are not options but obligations—which leads us to a final thought about the fate of the third servant in both stories.

Smug Security
and Creative Risk

The parable in Luke 19 is much more complicated in some ways. Unfortunately, many possible implications of both parables must be saved for another day because we are deliberately attempting not to overallegorize either parable.

The third servants in the two parables are almost identical.

They both shrugged off their responsibilities.

They both came up with a rather lame excuse (You are a hard man, sir!).

Both of them could have misappropriated the money, but they didn't (possibly due to their fear of their master —which, incidentally, is a terrible motive).

They both took some precaution with their capital.

They both were severely reprimanded.

In fact, their punishment hardly seems commensurate to the crime. This is why we must remember the content of the parables as well as the context.

These are not salvation parables. They deal with basically one subject: responsibility (individual and collective). The task of enlarging and enriching the Kingdom of God was given to the believers, although the fringe benefits spread far beyond the closed circle.

In this parable, these servants were not slaves or chattel. They were (and are) to be considered more as employees, at least in some sense committed to their employer. Jesus was not talking about responsibility given to unbelievers, but to believers.

The fate of the unfaithful servants must be understood in this light. It is true that they were deprived of the money which they had salted away. However, it was not their money. It was capital given to them by their employer to be invested during his absence. As mentioned before, when one shirks one's responsibility, someone else gets an extra burden. It was reasonable for the money to be taken away from the unfaithful servant and given to the most faithful one. The capital was given to the person who was most able to assume the added responsibility.

Then the parables again drift apart. In the first parable, the unfaithful servant was not only severely rebuked and had his responsibility taken from him, he was cast out into utter darkness where people weep and gnash their teeth (Matthew 25:30).

If this servant were truly a servant (and we have no reason to believe otherwise), we must interpret this passage accordingly. We could allegorize that there is a Judas in every crowd, but that's not the point.

The oriental way of describing estrangement and punishment would use very dark terms, exactly as Jesus did: outer darkness, weeping, and gnashing of teeth. But it does not necessarily follow that the third servant was cast into hell because he failed to fulfill his responsibility. Believers are not cast into hell for lying down on the job.

It does follow, however, that the third servant was relieved of the joy of his responsibility. There is hardly anything more miserable than to have the feeling of letting someone down—or accepting a responsibility and failing to do anything about it.

There is another curious wrinkle in these parables.

There might be a subtle suggestion of reward in the parable of the pounds which is not noticeable in the parable of the talents. The faithful servants in Luke's account were given charge over cities.

Some could argue that this is not a reward but punishment (who wants to be the mayor of a troublesome town?). Even so, it clearly speaks of an added responsibility given for faithfulness and, we might add, fruitfulness.

Could it be that Jesus is suggesting that there is no such thing as reward for good behavior in accepting responsibility, per se, but that the reward comes from the deep satisfaction that accompanies faithfulness and increased responsibility?

There is little contentment from monetary gain or political power, but there is a calm serenity from hearing

Smug Security
and Creative Risk

the Master say, "Well done, my good and faithful servant."
No reward can top this.

To the contrary, there is nothing but frustration
(gnashing of teeth), alienation (outer darkness), and regret
(weeping) in store for believers who are indifferent,
careless, indolent, too clever for their own good, or
captives of fear, who come up with lame excuses and add
to the burden of others. There is no happiness (or reward)
in smug security, but there is in creative risk-taking to
expand the Kingdom of God and spread the Good News.

CHAPTER THREE
PLANTING
GOD'S SEEDS
Matthew 13:3-23
Mark 4:3-20
Luke 8:5-15

Did Jesus give the explanation of his parable of the sower, or is it the work of a later editor?

Personally, I feel that the Scripture is clear. Jesus told the disciples what his parable meant. Why?

The poor disciples needed it. They were going crazy with the stories of Jesus which made sense, but not enough sense. They wanted to know not only why he spoke in parables, but what they meant. It was not only like Jesus to answer them, but he patiently explained one of the most obvious parables, showing how simple but subtle it actually was.

Early in the Christian era, interpretations of parables and other Scriptures were sometimes more imagination than interpretation. Jesus' own explanation of this particular parable was totally accurate and to the point and has become an exceedingly fine model for other interpretations.

Because Jesus spoke so much about seeds and the sowing of seed, it is apparent that he knew the subject well—and he knew that his listeners also knew the subject. No one, even if he lived in Jerusalem, was very far from Mother Nature (quite unlike the city slicker of today). Jesus used an appropriate subject most effectively. Even the farmer (and there must have been many in the crowd by the sea) understood the simple story, but knew no more of the hidden meaning than cynical professors from Jerusalem sent to mingle among the crowds and spy on the storyteller.

At first glance it might appear that these people didn't know much about farming. Ironically, they might have known more than we moderns think. We tend to smile (or even smirk) as we read, "Behold, the sower went forth to sow; and it came to pass that some seed fell by the wayside . . . on the rocky ground . . . and among the thorns . . ."

What a waste of seed! Imagine—a farmer scattering seed to the wind on top of ground that was hard as rock! He wasn't farming, he was feeding the birds. Think so?

This parable is a dramatic reminder that we must know the culture and the agriculture of the time before we can get at the message of the parables.

It is true that the sower threw seed—lots of it—on top of unplowed soil. It is also true that the wind blew some of it away, the birds got their share, and some landed on poor soil and in the brambles. In those days, as in ours, people didn't walk around a field if they could cut across. This meant that most fields had a crisscross pattern of hard pathways through them during the off-season.

After the seed was planted, not before, the farmer plowed the field. This was not only tradition, it was astute farming which some have found out the hard way after watching winds blow upturned soil skyward.[1]

---

[1] For a fascinating description of dry land farming, read James A. Michener's *Centennial*, "The Dry Lands" (New York: Fawcett World, 1976), pp. 731 ff.

45
Planting
God's Seeds

The farmer, before he scattered seed, knew that much of it would be wasted. He also knew that he had chances of getting thirty, sixty, and up to 100 bushels of grain for each bushel he scattered. He could afford to be generous, but not reckless.

No, he didn't throw the seed on the rocks, but on soil which covered the rocks. It was impossible in most cases to remove the pesky hidden rocks, and it was folly to attempt to mark the spots. He knew fully well that some of the seed would grow quickly and wither equally fast because the soil was thin. Some of the soil was so infested with brambles and weeds that he simply assumed a certain loss and lost no sleep over it.

The farmer was a blend of a fatalist (what will be will be) and a theist (I can plant, but I can't make it grow) as well as a pragmatist (I'll do what I can). What he could do was recognize the fact that for centuries the rains came and went in a more or less regular pattern. He had a built-in almanac which told him not to expose the good soil to the maddening wind, but to turn the soil upward when the moisture below would do the most good.

These farmers did not hold rain dances (or even prayer meetings) when the rains stopped prematurely, nor did they sell all the grain because the price was high only to panic at seed time. Common sense prevailed, although it was undoubtedly somewhat tormented at times by indolence, greed, and myopia.

Now perhaps is the time to compare city parables with country parables.

A glance at all of the parables of Jesus quickly reveals a rural or at least small-town milieu (thus his emphasis on agriculture, simple living, etc.). In fact, there was little city life in the career of Jesus. He was much more at home in the country, small towns, the lake region, and the desert. So were most of the people.

It is only recently that inhabitants of planet earth have squeezed themselves into cities. It has been said that in 1800 about 3 percent of the world's population lived in cities. That rose to about 13 percent during the next century, and it is only suddenly that the cities have grown unmercifully so that, alas, we live in an urban world with all of its complexities (and idiocies).

What used to be common knowledge escapes countless persons today. Many have never known the sweet scent of newly mown hay or the pungent smell of a barn.

Amazingly, the homey illustrations used by Jesus are still appropriate—with a little explanation now and then —to everyone.

However, spiritual understanding doesn't come easily for the city dweller, who is not often dependent on the sun and rain for his livelihood (at least not directly). This breeds the attitude of "Who needs God when I've got me?" Jesus had to cut through this attitude then as he does now and chose to do so with simple, earthy, ordinary, everyday life situations which, although most common to rural folk, are universal in their appeal as well as application. The parables speak equally well to city slickers and country folk.

The ancient wise man put it bluntly: "Go to the ant, you sluggard." Jesus said, "Go to the farmer."

Because this parable is self-explanatory, it is unnecessary to repeat and impossible to improve the interpretation.

However, there are some other dimensions which ought to be considered. The most important one, perhaps, is the ambiguous answer given by Jesus to the question, Why do you talk in parables?

"For to him who has will more be given, and he will have great plenty; but from him who has not, even the little he has will be taken away. That is why I use these illustrations, so people will hear and see but not understand," said Jesus (Matthew 13:12, 13, TLB).

Many interpretations of Jesus' words have been suggested, with varying degrees of insight. Perhaps a glance at the situation is in order.

Jesus, during the telling of this parable (and most others), was coming down the homestretch. His earthly mission was approaching twelve o'clock. He would soon lift his

feet from the earth and turn over the keys of the Kingdom
to Peter and the disciples. No longer would Jesus be
near to answer questions, silence critics, defend the
downtrodden, walk on the water, and turn water into wine.
Nor would he be able to teach his disciples, face to face,
any longer. This meant that what he did now, in a very real
sense, was to prepare them for graduation.

Jesus had been with his disciples for three years. During
this time he frustrated them often, bewildering them with
his radical approaches (drinking water with the Samaritan
woman, defending the prostitute but not her profession,
throwing verbal karate chops at smug theologians, and
falling asleep during treacherous storms at sea). It should
be remembered that he must have had hundreds and
thousands of conversations which have not been recorded
(the Bible is formidable enough without another 20,000
pages). The fact that we have a few parables kept intact
doesn't mean that these were all he told. However, we
must make the assumption that these are representative as
well as adequate for our twentieth-century spiritual
digestion.

Jesus no doubt told many more parables than we have
recorded. He also probably went into considerably more
detail than the written record reveals. When Jesus
explained why he talked in riddles (which is what many
of the parables were to the people as well as the disciples),
he gave some clues.

Although at best his answer to their question is a bit
vague, let's examine his answer with an attempt to find a
practical understanding even if not a philosophical one.

Jesus, why tell stories when you can teach so eloquently
in sermons and homilies, they probably reasoned. Jesus
was a master at oratory. His verbal debates speak for
themselves. His rhetorical questions were gems. His
conversational style was masterful. But here is Jesus,
telling amusing, earthy, and sometimes even embarrassing
tales. The disciples wanted to know why.

Consider the audience here. Jesus is speaking to a large
crowd in the great out-of-doors along the shores of the Sea

of Galilee. The crowd was enormous and stayed with Jesus
day after day.

It would be presumptuous to think that everyone in the
crowd hung on to every word Jesus spoke (no preacher or
orator, not even Jesus, enjoyed that luxury).

There were curiosity-seekers who followed every crowd
just as some people follow fire trucks.

Some followed simply because everyone was doing it.
They perhaps never heard of Jesus and had no idea why
such a crowd gathered, but they were there.

There were mothers with small children who ran about
the hillside and played at the water's edge.

There were retired folk who braved the hot sun to listen
to this new rabbi, wondering if perhaps he truly was the
promised One.

Teenagers, with not too much to do, joined the crowd,
and there were the menfolk who had finished sowing seed.

Mingled with the crowd were dignitaries from Jerusalem
who had been sent out to spy. The city fathers were
worried lest this wandering rabbi threaten the tranquillity
of the land or its religion.

Yes, it was an unusual gathering. Most crowds are.
Among these people Jesus had some friends, a few
enemies, and a great host of uncommitted—and
undecided. Before Jesus departed, many of them would
make firm commitments—but it would be naive to think
that all abandoned their former way of life to embrace the
radical life-style proposed by Jesus.

Here was a man who talked about lilies of the fields
which worried not about clothes or fashions. Here was a
man who talked about a farmer who sowed seed on good,
bad, and indifferent soil. Here was a man who stretched a
lad's lunch until it fed thousands. Here was a man who
meandered about the countryside with a small band of
disciples. Here was a man who could utter great orations
but told simple stories.

But he was a great storyteller. And everyone loves a good
story. It would have been folly for Jesus to give a rabbinical
exhortation on Mosaic law to this crowd of people glued to

Planting
God's Seeds

the side of a hill overlooking a beautiful body of water.
So he told stories, stories they could mull over, remember
easily, and tell to the townsfolk when they returned home.
Stories that would teach his followers but would confuse
those who spurned him. This is why Jesus told parables.

There were other reasons Jesus spoke in parables,
particularly toward the end of his earthly career.

Two opposing dangers threatened his ministry. The
people, tired of their political oppression, were looking
for a messiah—in one sense, any messiah—who would
restore freedom to their promised land (or at least improve
the situation). The timing, however, was not right, and
Jesus did not want to be coronated king of Galilee. It
would interfere with the planned program.

When a man walks on the water, turns water into wine,
makes the blind see and the lame walk—when he has time
for ordinary folk, speaks so they understand, and loves
children—something is bound to happen.

Jesus, unwilling to turn the crowds away, softened his
message into simple stories. These stories or parables
caused considerable interest because the people knew
there was something more to them than a simple tale. As
they talked among themselves, wondering just what Jesus
meant by seed choked by weeds and a sixty-fold harvest,
Jesus was buying precious time. His time had not yet come,
either to be crowned king or to be sentenced to death.

Meanwhile, within the same audience, there were cynics
from the city. They took notes; they listened but failed
to comprehend. They probably argued that this Nazarene
might be a bit eccentric, but hardly dangerous. The
parables of Jesus disarmed them while it was arming the
disciples and the crowds who heard him gladly.

It is at this point that the disciples discovered that they
could not fully understand the simple stories. They were
bewildered and asked for an explanation: "Why do you
speak this way and what do these parables mean?"

We are still asking these same questions. Let's examine
his answer.

Jesus reminded them that they were loyal disciples who

wanted to hear and understand—and they would, Jesus assured them. But he said there were simply too many who didn't have ears to hear. They heard what they wanted to hear—no more. They believed what they wanted to believe —no more.

Sowing seed is hard work. Preaching is hard work. Teaching is hard work. The one who warned against throwing pearls before swine was practicing what he preached.

It simply was not wise or prudent to teach, exhort, plead, or take a crowd where it didn't want to go. Therefore, Jesus refused to exhaust himself by pleading his noble cause to people who merely wanted him to feed them when they were hungry, lift them up when they fell down, give them water when they were thirsty, and heal them when they went lame. This was not his major task.

Jesus wouldn't knuckle under to the temptation to merely woo the crowd. Rather, he wanted to teach his followers.

But in teaching in parables, Jesus also frustrated his critics, defused their verbal time bombs, and at the same time gave them a lot to think about as they plodded unmerrily back to Jerusalem, deeply perplexed and thoroughly outwitted.

In other words, there was "method in his madness."

Let's take a quick look at some of the implications of the parable of the sower.

Probably the most important point Jesus was making is this: Without the sowing of seed there will be no harvest; without someone to sow the seed, there will be no sowing; but no matter who does the sowing, and no matter where it is done, the results will not be identical. In fact, the results will range from nothing to fantastic.

In another parable, overlooked much too often (Mark 4:26-29), the point is made specifically. After the farmer sows the seed, he cannot make it grow. The sower in Mark 4 sowed the seed and then took off, knowing there was nothing more he could do. The seeds grew without his help. This is important. We have no option: our task is to sow seed. But the burden is no longer ours. Either it will grow or not. The responsibility, however, picks up again after the seed has begun growing.

The farmer was generous but not reckless with his seed. Yes, the wind took some and blew it off course (but it might be possible to choose a less windy day—or a better time of day). But nowhere do we read that the farmer sowed seed on rooftops or hard roadbeds. There are some places— usually rather obvious—where it is futile to sow seed. On the other hand, it is a good idea to sow seed even when it may be risky. Some of the seed fell among thorns and on thin soil. Perhaps this tells us that the sower must not try foolish impossibilities, but he also must not plant seed only in the safest, most promising ground.

For those who have difficulty with the interpretation that it is the devil who snatches away the planted seed (Jesus himself said this), it might be argued that the task of the devil is precisely this: to rob people of a personal faith.

Jesus knew from firsthand experience what he was up against—and what we are up against. The parable does us a favor by reminding us that we do not fight merely against the wind and the rain. Or against flesh and blood. We struggle against principalities and powers, the rulers of this world of darkness—we fight against a spiritual wickedness dedicated to devour every seed that is sown, if possible.

Fortunately, it is not possible. Although it is true that Satan is alive and well, busily occupied in the "unfarming" business, there is one more parable dealing with seeds that ought to be mentioned: that of *the mustard seed.*

This short story is crucial (you'll find it in Matthew 13:31, 32; Mark 4:30-32; Luke 13:18, 19). Not only is there a chance of hundred-fold growth, there is the potential of a tiny, insignificant, almost invisible seed growing into a huge bush-like tree in which many birds can make their home.

The Good News has been sown, and sown well. The Kingdom has been expanded to all the far corners of the earth, and its message translated into many tongues. The

vigilant seed-picker has been at work too; but thanks to
the generosity of the sowers, far too many seeds have been
planted. That, too, is good news.

CHAPTER FOUR
**THE GOD WHO
DOESN'T MEDDLE**
Luke 15:1-32

There is a considerable difference between *interference* and *influence*. To interfere means to hinder or impede; or put another way, to intrude or meddle. It is not a pleasant word, and it is overcast with a heavy negativism.

To influence means to indirectly (or intangibly) affect a person or course of events, to have power over someone or something.

Historically, mankind has been preoccupied with this problem. Does God intervene in the everyday activities of his creation; does he meddle in our affairs? Does God hold some mysterious power over us—a power of restraint on the one hand and a persuasive power on the other? If so, is this irresistible? Can God be persuaded himself? If so, how?

On the other hand, is God more or less nonchalant over

the course of events, allowing mankind and nature to act and interact, to rise and fall as the tide—with a minimum of divine intervention (or none at all)? This chapter, as we shall see, wrestles with this problem.

What is mankind's basic problem? Jesus said we are lost. He told the religious leaders of his time and place—when they criticized the company he kept—that he associated with sinners because they were lost and needed to be found. These religious leaders, as with some religious leaders of today, may not have known they were lost. Therefore, without meddling in their affairs or tampering with their theology (at this point), Jesus told them three simple stories.

Jesus did many things that caused anguish. On this particular occasion, the religious leaders were upset because Jesus was rubbing shoulders with "untouchables." He was fellowshipping with people who were obviously out-of-bounds.

For a rabbi in good standing, this would be a terrible breach of etiquette. Jesus, as a religious leader himself (he was a self-educated rabbi of increasing distinction), should have had no dealings with these despicable people. But here he was, not only associating with them, but eating their food in their homes. These religious leaders wanted to know why, and presumably they listened politely, if not impatiently, as Jesus told them another of his now famous parables.

The first part of the parable (actually a parable in its own right) was somewhat of a warm-up, in a way. He asked an innocent enough rhetorical question: If a shepherd had a hundred sheep and one of them got lost, wouldn't he leave the ninety-nine in a safe place and go looking for the one that was lost?

Jesus continued. This time he told them about a woman who had ten silver coins, but lost one of them. Again the question: Wouldn't she turn the house upside down until she found it?

In both cases, that which was lost was sought until it was found.

The God Who Doesn't Meddle

Then Jesus was ready for the clincher. He told about a man who had two sons. One of them left home and got lost.

But now Jesus changed his strategy. He didn't ask a rhetorical question: Wouldn't the father drop everything and go looking for his wayward son? Instead, Jesus continued the son's story.

He told about the inheritance, the journey to a distant country, the son's dissipation of body and soul, the hunger and loneliness, the humiliation of eating the same food fed to swine, and the excruciating pain of swallowing pride, composing a speech of forgiveness, and bending low in agonizing penitence. What a picture Jesus painted!

We do not know what the religious leaders thought of the extended parable because the episode ends with the telling of the story. We don't know whether or not they got the message.

What we do know is that Jesus vindicated himself as he explained to them why he associated with the riff-raff of the community.

Each "parable of the parable" has a happy ending. The shepherd called his friends and neighbors to celebrate his good news. The woman called her friends and neighbors in for a cup of coffee as she told them about turning the house upside down until she found the silver coin she had lost. The father threw a party—and what a celebration it was. This was quite a homecoming for a prodigal who had been dead but was alive again.

The message here is clear: there is cause for celebration when one person who is lost is found. That's why Jesus ate with the sinners of the city—not necessarily because he enjoyed their company, but it was his way of seeking to save those who were lost.

We sometimes justify our questionable associations, but for the wrong reason. Too often we eat, drink, and make merry as an end rather than as a means to an end, hoping perhaps that our association might have some kind of leavening influence. If Jesus were here today, chances are he would attend some wild office parties and cocktail hours, but on his terms.

Notice the interesting mathematical development in this extended parable.

There were 100 sheep, ten coins, two sons. In each case, one was lost. With some interpretative gymnastics there are countless possibilities to establish an explanation. However, again we must caution ourselves that this is a parable, not an allegory. It is therefore unnecessary to find a rationale for the numbers Jesus chose.

Even so, let us examine one possibility.

In the case of the missing sheep, nothing is said about how the sheep got lost. The implication seems to warrant, however, this explanation: most sheep that get lost simply wander away from the flock. There is nothing to suggest that it was deliberate. Sheep, like humans, are inquisitive, tend to meander about, and sometimes drift away from the leader. In all likelihood, the sheep either wandered into a thicket or fell into a crevice where it was trapped, helpless unless rescued by the shepherd.

This is not the situation in the story of the missing coin. Actually the coin had nothing to do with getting lost. That was the fault of someone else who, either through carelessness or by accident, caused the coin to get lost.

However, in the last story of the parable, the wayward son falls into a different category. His act was premeditated, deliberate, and carefully planned.

Jesus seemingly was stressing something here in his unique choice of three different situations. Could it be that in the situation of the sheep, where he used a large number, 100, Jesus might be suggesting this: of all who have gone astray, the largest number go astray as sheep, without much forethought; they go their own way until they are hopelessly lost. Most of us probably fall into this category.

However, there are others of us who are lost not through the fault of ourselves, but because of the carelessness of others. Some children, when reviewing their situation, hardly had a chance. Others have been exposed to a climate where the nurture of the Christian faith was virtually hopeless. Admitting that everyone shoulders a certain responsibility for himself, there are situations—though far fewer in incidence—where someone else bears considerable responsibility for one who is lost.

In the last situation, there are only two cases, not ten or 100. The prodigal son is an amazing caricature of the human predicament. There are some—perhaps only a few in number by comparison—who engineer their own doom.

Not many of us have said, in effect, "I'm going to do whatever I want to do. If there is a God, I dare him to strike me dead!" But countless of us have, like sheep, gone astray, each one to our own way.

Jesus was talking to self-righteous religious leaders— men who without doubt were lost (but didn't know it?)— and would be categorized by one of these figures of speech.

As religious leaders, they might simply have drifted away from the truth of the teaching they proclaimed without fully realizing it. Or they might have inherited a hardened, rigid position and merely perpetuated it. Or they might have deliberately been squandering their spiritual inheritance.

At any rate, Jesus told these religious leaders that he was associating with the sinners of the city, not because he needed them, but because they needed him—because they were lost and in need of someone who would find them.

He told the religious leaders that they were lost too—and that people get lost in different ways. In fact, implied Jesus, that is exactly what he is all about. Jesus came to seek and to save those who are lost because everyone, like a sheep, or a coin, or a prodigal son, has gotten lost—one way or another.

This brings us to a monumental question—the question which was raised earlier in the chapter: why did the shepherd go looking for the lost sheep, and the woman turn the house upside down searching for the coin she had lost, but the father did not go looking for his wayward son?

If, and certainly they must be, these stories are illustrative of the heart and mind of the Savior of the world, Christ himself, could it be possible that in some cases God goes looking for the lost and in other cases the lost must look for himself?

Or is it the eternally agonizing question of maintaining a delicate balance between irresistible grace and man's responsibility? The shepherd sought until he found, but the father waited for the son's return.

Without attempting to easily solve the deep mysteries of God's grace and man's responsibility—which are hardly mutually exclusive—there is something afoot in these stories which demands our pursuit.

Could it be that the Good Shepherd will go to any end to seek and save one sheep that has gone astray? Could it be that the one which is lost is that important? The answer obviously is affirmative. We even sing about it:

*Jesus loves the little children,
All the children of the world:
Red and yellow, black and white,
All are precious in His sight.
Jesus loves the little children of the world.*

Soloists, choirs, and congregations have sung hundreds of songs about the Good Shepherd and various renditions of the Twenty-third Psalm. Notice the words of this hymn:

*There were ninety and nine that safely lay
In the shelter of the fold,
But one was out on the hills away,
Far off from the gates of gold—
Away on the mountains wild and bare,
Away from the tender Shepherd's care.*

*"Lord, Thou hast here Thy ninety and nine;
Are they not enough for Thee?"
But the Shepherd made answer: "This of Mine
Has wandered away from Me,
And although the road be rough and steep,
I go to the desert to find My sheep."*

*But none of the ransomed ever knew
How deep were the waters crossed;
Nor how dark was the night that the Lord passed through
Ere He found His sheep that was lost.*

59
The God Who
Doesn't Meddle

Out in the desert He heard its cry—
Sick and helpless, and ready to die.

"Lord, whence are those blood-drops all the way
That mark out the mountain's track?"
"They were shed for one who had gone astray
Ere the Shepherd could bring him back."
"Lord, whence are Thy hands so rent and torn?"
"They're pierced tonight by many a thorn."

But all through the mountains, thunder-riv'n,
And up from the rocky steep,
There arose a glad cry to the gate of heav'n,
"Rejoice! I have found my sheep!"
And the angels echoed around the throne,
"Rejoice, for the Lord brings back His own."

These two songs point out the love and compassion of the
Good Shepherd as well as the exhausting struggle involved
in seeking, finding, and saving the lost. The lost are not
easy to find at times, nor are they easy to save. It often
involves long hours of weariness and frustration, no matter
where they are lost—whether it be out in the dark,
dangerous, mountainous wilds or in the cozy warmth of
the house.

Consequently, in some situations everything comes to
an abrupt halt while the search goes on for the lost—even
one that is lost. But in others, everything continues—more
or less—in the same way while the lost is going deeper
into the wilderness. The prodigal son kept getting more
and more lost—if it can be put that way. Even so, no one
came looking.

The father didn't come himself. He didn't send a servant.
He didn't send the reluctant brother, who in his own way
was hopelessly lost in the comforts of his own home.

Why didn't the father go looking for his son? What was
Jesus trying to say? This is an extremely difficult question
—but an important one.

It is certain that if Calvin and Arminius, probably the
two foremost proponents of the antitheses found in this
extended parable, were unable to settle the issue of God's
responsibilities vs. man's, we might not be able to do much

better. In spite of the debates, remonstrances, and counter-remonstrances,[1] the question still faces us in this parable: why did the shepherd go looking for the sheep, but the father did not go searching for his son? Are we confronted with the dual role of the Savior of mankind—a Savior who searches diligently for the lost and a Savior who waits lovingly and patiently for the lost to come home? The answer is yes.

In the first place, a sheep caught in a thicket or lying at the bottom of a crevasse cannot possibly get back to the sheepfold. Nor can the other sheep help one found in this predicament. Only a shepherd can save him. Sometimes we glibly say that "God helps only those who help themselves" which is a half-truth at best, but untruthful in this context.

Calvin was correct: man cannot save himself.

This is also seen in the next phase of the lesson Jesus is teaching. The coin could not find itself. Even worse, the coin didn't know it was lost. In fact, the coin didn't even know it was a coin—that it had value. Only the owner knew that. Here is another important point. Not only do some fail to realize their lost condition—they have no idea of their worth. In God's sight everyone is valuable. Every single person is lost, but God is not willing that any should perish.

If we had only these two dimensions of this extended parable, we might be inclined to say that Calvinism, as popularly understood, is absolutely right and Arminius was wrong in challenging this position. However, we read on into the text about a son who was lost—very much so— but his father seemingly does nothing about it. Why didn't he go looking for his wayward son? Or at least send someone else out looking?

There are many possible reasons. The son, we must

---

[1]After Jacobus Arminius (1560-1609) died, his followers summarized his ideas in the Remonstrance, basically stressing the concept of free will (and human responsibility). Calvinists responded with the Counter Remonstrance which set forth the basic ideas of Calvinism (the sovereignty of God, irresistible grace, etc.).

remember, was in a position where he could, if he wanted to, do something about his own salvation. The sheep and the coin could not help themselves.

Furthermore, the son deliberately chose to do what he did. Perhaps he didn't realize all the consequences, but he certainly went against his upbringing. He probably was well schooled in moral matters and presumably was brought up in a religious climate.

Then, too, the wise father knew that if his son found out the hard way, he might be all the richer for it. He might have known the temperament of his son as well and determined not to interfere, hoping that the son would come to his senses. Remember: "a person convinced against his will is of the same opinion still." God doesn't coerce or meddle.

No matter how we look at it, a certain amount of self-responsibility was involved in the son's situation.

Consequently, we see a vivid picture of God's nature (searching and waiting) as well as man's nature (lost because of carelessness or rebellion and lost because of the fault of someone else). These, regardless of one's theology, seem to be the hard facts of life.

I don't want to conclude this chapter without going into even more depth on what is probably the most ingenious, poignant, and beloved of all the parables, the parable of the prodigal son(s).

One way to do this would be to retell the parable—in the light of the above—not with the view of telling it better, which cannot be done, but to bring out some aspects which could possibly be overlooked.

Once upon a time a certain man had two sons. This father was an unusual man, although we could say that his sons were rather normal—or at least typical. One day, probably because of his resentments and restlessness, the younger son asked to get his inheritance in advance.

The father, who by tradition and nature had planned to provide well for his family, reluctantly agreed, seemingly knowing what the son had in mind. When the son had his inheritance put into cash, he took off, not for the nearest town but for a distant and probably exotic—at least to him —country. There he became extremely popular, as long as he had money. But after spending freely, even recklessly, he eventually went broke. When he no longer had money, he discovered that he no longer had friends.

Hard times fell on the country, and in desperation he accepted the only means of livelihood available. He, a young man reared to avoid swine for religious as well as health reasons, found himself employed feeding pigs. A most desperate occupation, but what else could he do?

He had only two alternatives: he could stay or he could go home. But he couldn't stay. There was something within him which drove him to rebel against his current state of affairs. There had to be a way out of his self-made predicament.

He remembered his life at home. He pictured what the servants had to eat, and debated whether he should eat the pods he fed the pigs. Finally he decided to go back home. But it was an agonizing decision.

He planned his return journey carefully, rehearsing the speech he would give when he met his father: "Father, I have sinned against heaven and against you. I am no longer worthy to be your son; treat me no longer as a son, but as one of your servants."

The young prodigal never had a chance to use his carefully worded speech. He had gotten only part way through it when his father smothered both his son and the words in a passionate embrace. Then the father delivered the speech he had been practicing for a long time, wondering if he would ever be able to use it.

Calling his servants, he said, "Bring quickly the best robe we have, and put it on my son. And put shoes on his feet and a ring on his finger. Then prepare a banquet with the calf I've been fattening for this celebration. We're going to eat and celebrate like we've never celebrated before, because my son who was dead is alive." And they began immediately to make merry.

The robe, shoes, and ring made it clear that the son was fully restored as son again. The father did not ask for an

explanation or an alibi. Besides, there wasn't any. All
was forgiven and forgotten.

However, the other brother—older and presumably
wiser—was working away from the house and didn't know
that his younger brother had returned. Inquiring about
the reason for the celebration, he heard the disturbing
news: his kid brother, the prodigal, had returned.

His was a human reaction. Very human. He knew what
his brother had been doing. In the long run, there are no
secrets. The elder prodigal refused to have anything to do
with the celebration. He wouldn't even enter the house,
causing his father to go out and beg him to reconsider.

He was adamant in his refusal, reasoning self-
righteously, "Look, father, all these years I have served
you faithfully. I have never disobeyed you, nor have I
made a fool out of you like this other son of yours. Knowing
what he did, how can you celebrate like this?"

Obviously pained with a heavy heart, the father
answered simply, "Son, your brother got nothing that
rightfully belonged to you. But your brother was dead and
now he is alive again. Come on, let's celebrate!"

There the parable ends.

Jesus had finished talking to the religious leaders,
answering the question which was disturbing them.

Did they realize that Jesus was God's Son who came into
the world, not to condemn, but to seek and save that which
is lost? Did they realize that he would not force any of
them against their will? Had they forgotten the words of
their ancient prophet Isaiah:

All we like sheep have gone astray; we have turned every
one to his own way; and the Lord hath laid on him the
iniquity of us all. (Isaiah 53:6, KJV)

As these self-righteous leaders went their way, no doubt
they pondered the words of Jesus—over and over again.

The *lost sheep*: wandered away, hopelessly lost,
helpless without a shepherd to seek until he finds even if
the going is rough.

The *lost coin*: lost but didn't know it, nor did it know it had value, but was found only after an agonizing search, not far away but right at home.

The *lost son*: lost because of a deliberate, premeditated act and no one went looking . . . found when he came to his senses, repented of his deeds, and returned home—seeking retribution but finding forgiveness.

The *lost brother*: stubborn, proud, self-righteous, bitter, cynical, but basically a pretty good fellow . . . on the inside looking out and on the outside looking in, which is where he still is perhaps.

The *waiting father*: forgiving, hopeful, patient, sensitive, realistic . . . refusing to intrude or meddle.

These words are still haunting the human race whenever they are pondered. It's bad news when we're lost and can't do anything about it—or when we're lost and aren't aware of it—or when we're lost and don't do anything about it. But it's good news when we are found.

CHAPTER FIVE
**THE CREDIBILITY
OF DEPRAVITY**
Luke 10:25-37

A burning question was handled in an amazing fashion in this parable: how good are good people and how bad are bad people?

Or it can be put this way, too: how good are bad people? Or, how bad are good people?

These are not tongue-twisters or double-talk. These are very profound questions and they have formed the basis for countless debates down through the ages.

There are those who argue that man is basically good but is somewhat corrupted by his environment, and perhaps a little by his heredity. Others disagree and claim that man is inherently evil with occasional seizures of virtue.

This incident sheds some light on this controversy. It began with a lawyer (a religiously educated scholar whose role was to interpret the law in times of dispute), who seemingly was a spokesman for a delegation sent to probe into the theology of Jesus.

The lawyer stood up to address Jesus with a phony question. He was not interested in finding out how to inherit eternal life, but he was interested to hear what Jesus would say. Then, as a lawyer, he would have some hard evidence on which to hang Jesus. As it turned out, Jesus was hung later, but on "soft" evidence.

In effect, this is what the lawyer was saying: "We have heard many things about your teaching, Jesus. Since we haven't had the privilege of hearing from you personally, would you mind answering a couple of questions? What should I do to inherit eternal life?"

Jesus simply did what he often did: he answered the question with a question. "You are an expert in the law. What does the law say about this? How do you interpret it?"

The lawyer wasn't expecting to answer his own question, but because this was his area of expertise, he gave an excellent answer. He displayed some gems from the ancient Mosaic law and answered correctly, with precision. Jesus was impressed and congratulated him. What he had said was true. Anyone who loved God with his whole heart, soul, strength, and mind and loved his neighbor as himself would find eternal life waiting for him. Regrettably, this is hardly possible—but not everyone knows it, or admits it.

Jesus did not get shipwrecked on the rocks of legalism. He was not advocating salvation by works. He simply was saying that anyone who is perfect has no need of salvation. Eternal life is guaranteed.

By now the balance of power had shifted from the lawyer to Jesus. Unwilling to lose face, the lawyer came up with another loaded question: "And who is my neighbor?"

It is difficult to say what the tone of voice was. Was it tinged with sarcasm? *And just who is my neighbor?* Was it a philosophical inquiry? Or was it blurted out—the first thing that came to his mind? Perhaps the words poured forth on the wings of a smile as he thought of his cleverness.

This time Jesus didn't ask him what he thought. Instead, he went into one of his charmingly devastating parables. There was a lot at stake here, and Jesus took the opportunity not merely to dismantle a shrewd lawyer (although that he did), but to shatter the pomposity and hypocrisy of the religious community, individually and collectively.

Jesus, in this parable, showed the desperate condition of the human race as well as the insensitivity of the religious community in doing anything about it. The clergy of the world bear an enormous responsibility in helping redeem a battered and bruised humanity, and those who take the easy way out run smack into the wrath of God.

First, a look at some bad bad people.

A certain man was on his way down from Jerusalem to Jericho. This well-traveled road was a dangerous road as it twisted and turned giving would-be bandits every advantage. Sure enough, some robbers jumped the lonely traveler, stripping him of his belongings. But it was not enough to take what he had; they senselessly beat him and left him lying half-dead on the road.

Evil is ever present in this world of ours, but this kind of overkill represents another kind of viciousness. There are the Robin Hoods who take from the rich to give to the poor ... and there are those who rob to support an expensive addiction ... and some steal because they think they have it coming ... and there are those who steal for the fun of it or because it poses a challenge. But when a person is robbed and then beaten maliciously, we see another face of depravity.

Jesus was underscoring the predicament of man. The poor traveler, alone, jumped by a gang of thugs, was hopelessly outnumbered. Immediately Jesus had the empathy of the lawyer. It would have been virtually impossible for anyone not to see the gross injustice done.

We live in a world of "bad guys," and unfortunately

there are even worse people, the bad "bad guys." This is one form of depravity credibility.

Next, a look at some bad good people.

The lawyer, probably impeccable in the sight of his fellowmen, was hardly prepared for the next stage of the parable. Jesus was merciful and tactful. He could have said there was a certain lawyer going down to Jericho, but he didn't. Besides, the imagery is better using a priest.

The priest was evidently traveling alone when he came upon the victim's body lying on the side of the road. He paused, studied the situation momentarily, and continued on his way. But why?

One logical explanation could be that he was in a hurry to get home (many priests chose to live in Jericho). Others might say that he was in a hurry for an appointment (probably quite unlikely unless he were traveling toward Jerusalem). The priest might be defended by saying that he thought the poor fellow was dead and therefore needed a mortician rather than a priest. Or one could reason that the priest dared not touch the body for fear of being defiled, which would put him out of service for seven days. Lastly, though we could go on, some would suggest that it would be dangerous to stop since the bandits might be lurking nearby.

Whatever the reason—fear, lack of compassion, busyness, or a time factor—the priest failed to live up to the responsibility of the priesthood.

Jesus continued the story. The next person to come along was a Levite. He too sized up the situation and went on his way, possibly for the same reasons, more or less. The Levite, because of his religious occupation, likewise would be expected to stop and lend a helping hand.

Whether or not clergymen—rabbis, priests, pastors, or whatever—like it, they have something in common. There are certain expectations which they cannot shove aside. If anyone traveling that lonesome, dangerous road should have stopped—in the minds of people—it should have been a priest or a Levite.

The point is well made. A good person would have stopped in spite of an inconvenience or even danger.

The Credibility of Depravity

Even so-called good people are not always good.

But why would Jesus use both a priest and a Levite? Wouldn't one or the other have been adequate?

Jesus was talking to a religious leader, a lawyer by trade, who probably was a spokesman for the religious leadership of his time. Therefore, what Jesus had to say to the lawyer he also said to the religious community at large. A priest was a Levite, true; but not all Levites were priests. Jesus was not only speaking of the formal clergy (the priest) but the entire religious hierarchy (the Levite).

The tribe of Levi had been chosen to be the people through whom God would minister to his people. They were set aside and supported by the other tribes, not because they were superior, but because it freed them to perform their tasks. Today the clergy is patterned pretty much this way.

From the tribe of Levi came the priests, direct descendants of Aaron. They had specialized responsibilities directly related to worship and sacrifice.

On the other hand, the Levites served in many various roles, many of which were indirectly related to worship and sacrifice. Their function included administrative tasks, teaching, assisting, and writing. They also performed various physical tasks, serving as shepherds, tending cattle, and doing other sundry jobs.

In a simple but ingenious story, Jesus indicted the whole range of humanity—from wanton treachery on the one hand to subtle insensitivity on the other. Here we see unrighteousness at its ugly worst and hypocritical self-righteousness at its best (which is really its worst). Jesus was underscoring the plight of mankind by using examples of both extremes.

But he was doing more than that. He was saying that depravity is a fact, though not all depravity is obvious. Some of the evil of mankind—indeed perhaps the most diabolical—stems from the least expected quarters, and from those who ought to know better. This is a stern warning to the clergy of the world just as it is an indictment of behavior that is unneighborly, to put it mildly.

Finally, a look at a good bad person.

We have just seen what happens when certain responsibilities are denied. Now Jesus gave a new twist to his story.

After the priest and Levite had passed by, a solitary, despised Samaritan came along. Jesus couldn't have chosen a more *apropos* figure than a disliked, even hated neighbor to the north. Lest we scorn the Jewish lawyer and his clerical friends too readily, it must be said that the hostile feeling was mutual. The Jews and the Samaritans hated each other and avoided each other like a plague.

If Jesus wanted to teach neighborliness, he couldn't have found a better—or worse—way. His theology was radical: if your neighbor smites you on one cheek, turn the other and let him smite that one too . . . love your enemies and do good to those who despise you. Now he presented the least likely candidate as the neighborly person. In the minds of the religious hierarchy Jesus was dealing with, Jesus must have committed treason by showing the so-called bad Samaritan as the good Samaritan.

For those who wondered aloud if anything good could come out of Nazareth, what must they have thought about Samaria?

Up until this point in the parable, Jesus avoided detail. But now he poured it on (or perhaps rubbed it in). The decent Samaritan saw what had happened, ran the risk of getting jumped himself, dismounted, stooped to help the fallen man, and poured oil (to soothe) and wine (to disinfect) on the wounds. He then bandaged the injuries (perhaps taking portions from his own garments), set him on his own beast, and took him to a place where he would be cared for.

Not only that, he stayed with him overnight, paid in advance for several days' care, and promised to pay any balance when he returned.

This was the so-called good bad guy.

Was Jesus trying to tell them that neighborliness is often where you least expect it? Not really, although this certainly is often true. Was Jesus trying to tell the lawyer that neighborliness must go considerably deeper than he realized—or practiced? Yes, but that's not all.

The Credibility of Depravity

It is at this point that we must return to the original question. The lawyer, in trying to bait Jesus into an inappropriate answer, asked the ageless question: What must I *do* to inherit eternal life? Then the lawyer answered his own question: I must love God and my neighbor. Jesus simply but forcefully showed him that not only did he not love his neighbor; he actually despised and hated him.

Jesus knew that the lawyer wouldn't lift a finger to help a fallen Samaritan, and that the lawyer probably wouldn't lift a hand to help any fallen fellowman under similar circumstances (although he might help a fellow lawyer). Here, in dramatic terms, is depravity at its worst.

Is it any wonder that Jesus said that anyone who hates his brother (or neighbor) has no hope of inheriting eternal life? The lawyer gave the correct answer, but Jesus revealed the true meaning.

Although this parable certainly is a message about neighborliness, it is far more than that.

Jesus was telling us that eternal life, for the ungodly crook or the "godly" clergy, lies beyond reach. Eternal life can be inherited but only by those who can boast of perfection, those who keep the law in every aspect and love their neighbor—the unlovely as well as the lovely—as much as they love themselves. But alas, this kind of perfection—neighborliness coupled with high self-esteem —just doesn't exist.

The bad news is that the world is full of people who are unneighborly. But the bad news is even worse because there are those who abuse or neglect their high calling to minister to the needs of a battered and bruised humanity.

But there is good news too. There are good Samaritans who do minister to the needs of their fellowmen, who bandage broken bodies and bind up the brokenhearted.

Yes, there is even better Good News. It is possible to inherit eternal life through Jesus Christ because God so loved the world—the batterers and bruised, the haughty and self-righteous—that he gave his Son, so that whoever believes in him will not perish but have eternal life.

CHAPTER SIX
MANNERS AND MORALS
Luke 14:1-24

Some people have excellent manners but terrible morals. Others boast of high moral standards but are uncouth. Jesus had something to say to both.

Normally we expect boorish behavior from the dissolute and charming behavior from the righteous. But such is not always the case.

A charming, self-righteous Pharisee had planned a Sabbath dinner party with Jesus the honored guest. When Jesus arrived, he was ushered into a carefully planned dinner trap. There before him was another guest of honor, a non-Pharisee who was both obviously ill and ill at ease. The room was full of gawking Pharisees who were watching to see what Jesus would do.

The silence was as awkward as the ambush, until Jesus broke the mood with an abrupt question: "Is it lawful to heal on the Sabbath, or isn't it?" More silence.

Then Jesus acted. He took hold of the man, who was not fatally ill but looked rather pitiful (the Pharisees and lawyers weren't taking any chances that Jesus would overlook his illness), healed him, and let him go.

As much as this man wanted to be healed, he resented the way in which he was being used. Jesus, sensing this, made him whole again and then released him from this awful company. The man certainly wouldn't have enjoyed the dinner—these people didn't know how to extend a common courtesy to one obviously from another level of society. Besides, he would be anxious to show himself to his family and friends.

Jesus not only showed mercy; he displayed a marvelous sense of understanding and compassion, an essential ingredient of good manners.

Sensing that these boorish, sophisticated religionists needed another lesson or two in morals and manners, Jesus took the offensive again.

Here he simply used an illustration—perhaps even a parable in its own right—to amplify his meaning. "Which of you," he asked, "having a beast of burden (a means of livelihood) that has fallen into a well, will not immediately pull it out *even* (italics mine) on a Sabbath day?"

The loss of an ass or an ox would have been a major catastrophe at that time. However, the Pharisees and lawyers present did not make their living with a beast of burden, which is precisely why Jesus used this imagery. It was a part of his good manners. By referring to others, Jesus was able to make the necessary point without any needless offense. Tact and manners go hand in hand.

They were speechless, which is to their credit. Because Jesus had already won this round, it was futile for them to fight back—and foolish. Having good manners includes the capacity to keep silent at the right moment. And this was the right moment.

Sensing that the dinner trap was backfiring and might get completely out of control, the host evidently gave the word or the signal that dinner was ready. Talk about bedlam!

Everyone in the room (we can presume) had been to a dinner party before. But this time they violated their sense of protocol and literally scrambled all over each other to get to the highest places of honor at the table.

There is a positive relationship between etiquette and ethics. These men, religious leaders, prominent citizens, members of the elite ruling class, seemingly broke down completely in their wild scramble. What had happened? We do not know; we can only guess. But an educated guess would include the possibility that when they forgot their ethics, they also forgot their etiquette. This, incidentally, is a common malady.

Jesus, with a dramatic healing followed by an unanswerable question and another of his devastating illustrations, had literally shattered their reasoning power. Their diabolically conceived dinner trap had blown up in their faces, blinding them to all reason. Consequently, they acted by instinct, like animals, as Jesus stood nearby and watched with dismay.

It must have hurt Jesus to see this happen. Men of compassion, with high ideals and sensitive manners, do not enjoy seeing others make fools of themselves. Had Jesus been amused rather than troubled, he might have let it pass. However, good manners demand good judgment, and Jesus decided to take advantage of the opportunity to give another lesson on manners.

By now these religious leaders, embarrassingly exposed as quacks, hardly needed either an explanation or a scolding. Jesus decided against the scolding (except as it is implied) and went ahead with a simple, basic, almost unbelievably elementary description of basic protocol.

Again, Jesus used common courtesy and gracious tact. Choosing the disarming imagery of a wedding feast, Jesus told them:

If you are invited to a wedding feast, don't always head for the best seat. For if someone more respected than you shows up, the host will bring him over to where you are sitting and say, "Let this man sit here instead." And you, embarrassed, will have to take whatever seat is left at the foot of the table.

Do this instead—start at the foot; and when your host sees you he will come and say, "Friend, we have a better place than this for you!" Thus you will be honored in front of all the other guests. For everyone who tries to honor himself shall be humbled; and he who humbles himself shall be honored. (Luke 14:8-11, TLB)

Good manners and high morals disallow the temptation to gloat in the misfortune of others. Jesus was grieved because his fellowmen—lawyers and Pharisees, religious leaders—had made fools of themselves.

Yes, they knew better than to scramble for the seats of honor, but they did it anyway. Rather than let them brood in their embarrassing misery, knowing they had committed a grievous *faux pas*, Jesus did what good manners and high morals demand: he defused the situation. By telling this simple story, he reminded his dinner partners of their lack of consideration in a way that could hardly offend them. Everything Jesus said, they knew to be true—it was their way of life, their own code of ethics. Jesus exercised wisdom by not rubbing it in and displayed justice by not letting them get away with it. How to do both demands great discretion and compassion. Etiquette without discretion is not only ill-mannered; it is pernicious.

These men were supposedly the cultured, intelligent, respected, and above all, highly reputed men about town. If anyone knew and observed the existing pecking order, these men did. They knew who outranked whom because they did the ranking. Even so, Jesus did not debunk the system, hollow as it was.

Then again, in no way can it be said that Jesus justified their system of ranking people just because he rebuked them without destroying their routine. To the contrary, Jesus recognized the necessity of order and decency. He seemingly recognized that all men are created equal but some people outrank others, at least in the sight of men.

This is a curse and a blessing with which we must live.

Manners
and Morals

If there is no respect for persons of integrity, expertise, and even seniority, any system will break down. But when a society creates real and artificial barriers between people, caste systems and unnatural social strata emerge which can be and often are diabolical (or at least detrimental).

This is a tension with which we must live: recognizing the merits and weaknesses of those around us, and learning to respect (and even obey) mortal man.

Good manners can make harsh demands of us at times. Jesus did not leave us weaponless, however. Just in case his fellow table guests failed to get the message, he explained it: "Everyone who exalts himself will be humbled, and he who humbles himself will be exalted." There is the key that unlocks the mystery of manners and morals.

But there was more. As Jesus looked around the table and saw who the invited guests were, he gave a bit of advice to the host—privately or not we do not know. The advice, however, is public knowledge now—and what advice!

This man, who had certainly every right to invite whom he wanted to invite, evidently invited the same people over and over. There is nothing wrong with that, in a way, except that in this situation—and probably in many others as well—the invitations were becoming a culinary merry-go-round.

Here's how it worked. You would create your guest list, invite the prospects in ample time, create a cuisine they would enjoy, and then sit back and wait for the return invitation. This would be forthcoming, with an attempt, if not to upstage, certainly at least to equal the previous repast. After a few of these affairs, the fun would be gone, protocol would be more and more a burden, and soon the whole thing would merely be dull routine.

Why not, Jesus suggested, change your mailing list? Don't keep on inviting the same friends and relatives. Rather, invite people who never get an invitation: the poor, the lame, even the blind. They can't possibly repay you. Therefore, you'll have the blessing of doing something

without ever having to worry about being reciprocated.
Then when you have another dinner, invite another group
of people. It's true, they may not thank you, or they might
even be suspicious—but don't worry about that. You'll get
your reward someday, and what a reward it'll be. But
meanwhile, think of the great time you could be having.
Why not try it? I dare you!

Perhaps Jesus didn't sound like this, but then maybe he
did. No matter. What Jesus is suggesting is this: good
manners can break up little cliques before the cliques break
us up.

Christians have often lived with the tension of keeping
the right company and avoiding wrong associations. And
so we must to a point. Jesus could have saved himself
considerable grief by staying home that Sabbath day.
However, he went and we saw what happened. The same
will happen to us. Good manners sometimes will force us
into situations we would like to avoid. Good morals will
take care of us in these situations.

Inviting strangers, perhaps some with no manners,
might shatter our nerves and stain our carpeting—but
according to Jesus, it's worth the risk. One soul *is* worth
more than the whole world.

Enlarging our circle of friends could very well be an
ethical matter. It might be the only way to redeem someone
who is terribly lonely—and it could be a good way to
reduce our own snobbishness.

Jesus seems to be saying that protocol and good manners
are important, but not all-important. The guest list is also
important and should be revised regularly.

While Jesus was eating, a person sitting next to him—
who had heard the remarks Jesus had made—leaned over
to him and spoke. Perhaps it was the first time he addressed
Jesus and he was somewhat awed. Maybe he was trying to
make up for his previous behavior. Possibly it was merely
dinnertime small talk or a conversational opener. At any
rate, he might not have fully understood what he was
saying to the Lord.

Actually, it happens every day. If you go to dinner and

are seated next to a doctor, you talk about aches and pains.
If you are seated next to a musician, you talk about sharps
and flats. If you are seated next to an athlete, you try to
wangle a ticket to a big game.

This person was seated next to Jesus. Therefore, what
would he talk about? Aches and pains, sharps and flats,
free tickets? No. He would talk religion. He said, in effect,
"Won't it be great when we'll be able to eat together in
the coming Kingdom of God?"

Jesus could have said, "Yes, that'll be great," and kept
on eating. But Jesus is full of surprises.

Instead of brushing this pretentious clod aside (or was he
merely an awestruck dinner guest?), Jesus recognized by
the small talk that he hadn't understood a word he had
said. So Jesus kindly drew him—and the others at the table
—a verbal picture.

He told another of his indelible parables. He was not
willing that any should either fail to understand or
misunderstand. This included those who had set the
dinner trap as well as those who tried to display their
theological robes at the table. There was no direct rebuke,
no sigh, no exasperation, no smirk—nothing but another
story. Talk about manners!

In this story Jesus, sensing that he was not getting
through, shifted his attack from straightening out their
manners to rectifying their religion. Although religious
leaders in good standing—lawyers and Pharisees—their
theology was an outrage.

What better table talk is there than a pleasant yarn?
Having already talked about a wedding feast, Jesus kept the
imagery alive as he told of a man who created a gala feast
but no one came. Incredible breach of etiquette, actually,
because in those days any great dinner was a monumental
event. An invitation went out long before the scheduled
event—with an RSVP. Most of those invited would be
honored to accept. Then, shortly before the event, a
reminder went forth. This time it was a personal reminder
as one of the servants made the rounds.

In Jesus' story, one after another of the invited guests

began to make excuses. This was an unheard-of breach of etiquette. No one, absolutely no one, would accept the original invitation and then renege. By now everyone at the table was listening intently, identifying compassionately with the injured host.

Jesus carefully chose the illustrative excuses that were made. The first involved a person who had purchased a piece of land and wanted to be excused so he could go out and see it. Whether he bought it sight unseen (rather unwise) and wanted to verify it, or if he simply wanted to look it over so he could admire it, is uncertain. In either event, it was hardly a justifiable reason for breaking an important date.

The next example is equally unreasonable. A certain person bought five yoke of oxen and wanted to be released from his previous commitment so he could check them out. Again, did he buy them without proving them, or was he so enamored by them that he had to see how powerful they were as a team? Either way, he was unjustified. Had one of his oxen fallen into a pit, he would have been justified for begging a release from his commitment.

But Jesus is bending over backward to make his point: these are phony excuses, not valid reasons. His third illustration, however, is a little more challenging. This person had just married, and therefore could not come.

Here we must make some presumptions. First, perhaps he was single at the time of the invitation but was married before the banquet. Therefore, it would not be proper for him to attend without his wife. This would have been a greater breach of etiquette than breaking the banquet date, particularly in the light of marital life (and the honeymoon) in the first century. The first year following a marriage was considered especially sacred.

This, however, probably is not a valid reason because he would have known at the time of the banquet invitation that he was going to be married. This culture disallowed elopements and sudden ceremonies. It seems, then, that this man forgot his etiquette either by not declining the

original invitation or by not explaining what his marital
situation would be at the time of the gala affair. If he would
have wanted to go badly enough, he certainly would have
wanted his bride-to-be included as well. (It should be
noted that certain feasts were for men only. If this were one
of those occasions, this reasoning would not fit.)

Looking intently at the three prototype situations, we
probably can read into them three kinds of situations in
life which hinder us from accepting an invitation to the
Banquet of banquets and from accepting our full
responsibility before God.

The land is representative of possessions, and those
things which we acquire or strive after are among our
greatest stumbling blocks. Esau sold his birthright for a
bowl of soup, and we sell our souls often for even less.

The five yoke of oxen seem to typify our vocational
life, which too often overshadows more important matters,
including fellowship at dinner parties and elsewhere.
Why, Jesus said, should you be a slave to your job when you
could be out enjoying and interacting with people? The
moral is clear—people are more important than work,
especially in the matter of being one of the people of God.

Marriage is important to Jesus even though he never
married. In fact, marriage is God's idea and family life
demands and receives high priority. Even so, Jesus made it
very plain that not even marriage should be allowed to rob
a person of eternal life, for that is what this great Banquet
is all about. If we are not careful, we will miss out on
eternal life because of our possessions, occupations, or
domestic situations.

When the servant came back and reported what was
happening, the master became angry. The tables were set,
the food was prepared, the orchestra was tuning up, but
there were no people to enjoy it.

The servant was sent out again. This time he was
instructed to invite anyone and everyone to come to the
party. Still there was room. Again he went out, with
instructions to beat the bushes and compel or urge people

to come. The master was ready and wanted every place filled. But none of the ones who were invited but reneged would be there.

The parable ended here, right between a pleasant yarn and a blunt warning. The dinner guests, accustomed to stories and parables—a part of their culture—knew pretty well what Jesus was talking about, although they probably had to wait until later to unravel the complete mystery.

Jesus came to his own people but was rejected. However, the invitation went out to anyone and everyone to come to the great Banquet, the everlasting wedding feast. But those who rejected the invitation would not be recognized when they came knocking at the door. Over and over again Jesus bombarded the people with different figures of speech as well as direct confrontations so that they would know and understand his mission on earth.

What these dinner guests did with his table talk we do not know, except that shortly after this episode Jesus was condemned to death—probably by some of these same people who dined with him. It is a pity—for them—that they were offended both by his manners and his morals which were so foreign to them.

CHAPTER SEVEN
HOW NOT TO BUILD A HOUSE
Matthew 7:24-27
Luke 6:47-49

Jesus wound up his Sermon on the Mount with this clincher: "If you merely hear what I say, but don't practice what I preach, you are just like a person who built his house on the sand and then watched it wash away when the storms came."

Some years ago when we were traveling in Palestine on a desolate road, our guide took a moment to rest and sat down next to where I was sitting. After awhile, he pointed to a number of mud houses and said, "See those houses? They are all built on a riverbed. Every seven years or so, we have an unusually heavy amount of rainfall and that riverbed becomes a raging torrent. Every one of those homes will be washed away."

I found that hard to believe, partly because the houses looked as though they had been there forever. Before I could ask him if the people knew this would happen, he interrupted my thoughts with the answer, "They all know what will happen, sooner or later. When the heavy rains come, they simply pack up their belongings, move to higher ground, and when the storms are over go right back and build another house. People have been doing that for generations."

He went on to tell me that they have been advised—and even offered help—to build elsewhere, but evidently they like it that way.

My thoughts drifted thousands of miles to a house (one of many) located on the water's edge of the Mississippi, not far from Hastings, Minnesota, where the same thing happens. Every year, during the spring thaw, the river rises, inundating this house. Its occupants simply move out, and when the water recedes they rearrange the mud a little and move back in for another year.

Why do you suppose Jesus ended his now famous sermon with a parable about two builders? What is he trying to tell us?

Jesus had been talking to a huge crowd for presumably hours on end, day after day. In crowds such as this, there are many different types of listeners with an equal number of possible responses. Jesus was concerned lest they head home to forget everything they had heard.

He suspected that some would depart saying, "Wasn't that fantastic? Never before have I heard such an amazing storyteller." Jesus did not want to be known simply as a famous storyteller.

Others, he surmised, might go home, shake off the dust from their feet, and with it shake off the teachings and inspiration of the moment. Jesus did not want to be easily dismissed or forgotten; but he knew that unless these people practiced what he preached, that is exactly what would happen.

Jesus also probably sensed that some of the crowd would be so impressed that they would go home and not only repeat but dramatize what the country preacher had said and done. But Jesus was also afraid of this. He did not want

the people to become mere reporters. He wanted them to
become disciples, learners, loyal followers.

With this in mind, Jesus told this simple, easily
understood story (in that part of the world particularly).
It was the conclusion to a great sermon, a strategic moment
as Jesus clinched his message with a homey but immensely
important finale.

A word should be said at the outset about the two
builders and the location of the houses they built.

One builder was wise, the other foolish. He was foolish,
however, not because he built in a wadi but because he
built without a foundation. Since there are different kinds
of dry riverbeds, we can make the assumption that there
are some locations totally unsuitable for building under
any circumstance. However, this is not what Jesus is
suggesting.

A close reading of the text reveals that one house was
built on rock, the other on sand. But both were built where
they would be subject to the winds and the rain, a raging
torrent. In other words, they were built in the mainstream
of society where floods and storms do come and threaten
both the wisdom and craftsmanship of the builder. They
were not built in a safe place, a long way from the storms
of life. Life simply is not like that.

The message is quite clear. Those who heard the words
of Jesus would be subjected both to unpleasant, even
irksome flooding as well as disastrously cascading
torrents. Jesus wanted them to build, not where it was
pleasant and secure, but in a manner that could withstand
the worst storms of life. The only way to get a house like
this would be to build a good foundation under the house,
by going down to bedrock, by hauling in necessary
foundation stones. Then the house would be safe when the
pressure was on. Pondering what he meant, they drew their
own conclusions. No other pictures were necessary.

What had Jesus told them in this marvelous mountain-
side sermon? What was the foundation on which they
were to build their lives?

Jesus had told them that the poor in spirit will inherit

the Kingdom of God, that the sorrowing would some day be comforted. He said that peacemakers would be called sons of God and unjust persecution would not go unnoticed.

Jesus told his disciples that they were the light of the world and the salt of the earth. He cautioned them about discarding that which they knew and followed—their old law—and warned them about the hypocrisy of the scribes and Pharisees. Jesus also said that evil originates within the heart and then surfaces in the life.

This amazing itinerant preacher went on to say that they should love their enemies and do good to those who hate them. He even told them how to pray, and how not to pray. Jesus also reminded them that they have no real control over the future, but that the same God who takes care of the birds of the air and the flowers of the fields is even more committed to caring for people.

This same preacher said to ask and you'll find; and if your son asks a legitimate question, don't let him down. He warned them to look out for false prophets who are diabolically clever; but even so, he cautioned, "do unto others as you would have them do unto you."

These were foreign words to their ears and Jesus knew it. Their religion was external, and Jesus was trying to internalize it. It was impersonal, and Jesus was trying to personalize it. Their legalism was inadequate, and Jesus was trying to give them an adequate foundation for belief and life. Before they left him to face their everyday existence up in the village or down in the wadi, he wanted them to build their lives on these principles he had given them. Then, when either monotony or the storms of life swept through, the foundation would be there.

Yes, Jesus is saying that this news—the Good News—is more than news. It is life eternal.

There is another lesson here. Jesus is telling them—and us—not to take the easy way out.

Why did these villagers who repeatedly built in the wadi do so? One reason is that they took the easy way. After the storms had subsided, they knew that it would be years

How Not To Build A House

before another devastating flood would occur. Why not, they reasoned, rebuild as before? Everything they needed was there in the riverbed. From the clay they could fashion bricks, create the necessary mortar, and build the house which would protect them from the heat of the day as well as the chill of the night.

The mud would bake hard in the sun and would give protection against the wind, rain, and floods (except the occasional raging torrent).

They would not have to journey to higher ground, nor would they have to carry rocks or chip away at stubborn stones or dig down to safe bedrock. They could concentrate on living rather than building, which, suggested Jesus, is all too often the name of the game.

Even so, for these people who built and rebuilt over and over again, life was not entirely unspeakable. They did have shelter, they ate, drank, married and were given in marriage, and the heat of the day did not become intolerable nor were the nights unbearable. Why then, they could easily argue, spend so much time and energy on a foundation which shows so little for all the effort?

The world takes religion more or less for granted—but only as an add-on to life, not its foundation. The builders of society—unwise, to be sure—are so often preoccupied with the superstructure that little heed is given to the foundation. Wooden shake shingles and batten strips are much more important than the depth of the footing and the location of the drainage tiles. Cosmetics become all-important, and undue attention is given to bay windows and underground sprinkling systems. In this parable, Jesus is warning against building where it shows rather than where it counts.

Jesus knew that those who made up the great crowd on the hillside—at least the big majority—would return home where they would neither rob, cheat, nor kill. They would worship quite faithfully one day per week, make presentations of tithes and possibly even offerings in addition. They would pass on customs inherited from their ancestors, keep alive the arts of furniture-making and basket-weaving, and continue to bake unleavened bread and tramp in the vineyards.

These were not "bad" people. Their children were not malicious or evil. The next generation would follow more or less—mostly more—in the same footsteps. Tiny babies would be rocked quietly in loving arms. Heavy hands would nail rough lumber into boxes which would be lowered gently into mother earth's swelling bosom.

But this is not all there is to life, Jesus cried. There is a better way—a more abundant life, a richer life-style. That life, said Jesus, is not merely repeating yesterday today. The abundant life, yes, life eternal, is doing what the wise builder did: structuring life on a solid foundation.

The call to practice what he preached is the way Jesus ended every sermon. To hear, and even assent, is not enough.

CHAPTER EIGHT
THE RICH FOOLS
Luke 12:16-21
Luke 16:19-31

It could be said that there are two kinds of rich fools: those who put their riches in the bank and those who put their riches on their back.

These two parables are not usually juxtaposed with each other, but there is a sense in which they belong together.

The word "fool" is a fascinating word, particularly when you look at some of the synonyms: buffoon, clown, dunce, halfwit, idiot, jester, nincompoop, simpleton—or at some of the slang expressions: bonehead, chump, dummy, fathead, jackass, knucklehead, meathead. When God called the rich farmer a fool, which of the above—if any —did he have in mind? Whichever, it was a strong word which seems to combine an element of ignorance (or mindlessness) with egotism.

Rich people have all sorts of difficulty; not the least is

the anguish of getting richer. That was the problem with the well-to-do farmer in Luke 12 because he had had an exceptionally good year.

With a bumper crop staring him in the face, what were his alternatives? His storage barns were already full, which meant he would have to either build new ones or enlarge what he had. He tore the old down and built new ones, larger and doubtlessly improved.

Seemingly he could have lived well with what he already had and fed the hungry from his bumper crop. Perhaps this never occurred to him, but if it did, he promptly erased it from his mind. Why? The text explains why: he wanted to retire in wealth and ease (which he already could have done, but now he wanted to doubly insure his future prosperity).

Although a fool, this man was not a simpleton or a "meathead." His decision was a wise one, from a pragmatic point of view. Old barns always carry a much greater risk from leakage, rodents, etc. than new ones do. Besides, boneheads usually do not plan well for retirement, and halfwits are unable to. Therefore, his title of fool was earned elsewhere.

Part of his folly was that he worked so hard for so little: to take life easy. Years (or even weeks or months) of this kind of retirement take so much from a retiree and give so little. His last years could have been spent much more wisely.

Now it must be asked, Is there anything wrong—or foolish—with taking it easy at retirement? Part of the answer is found in homes for the elderly, and in cemeteries. The answer is both yes and no. It's OK to enjoy the fruit of many years of labor—as long as you can also look beyond that. This ambitious, hardworking farmer was a fool to think that the ultimate in life is to lay down the pitchfork and cuddle up on a soft sofa with a box of chocolates and a good mystery story. He had forgotten to reckon with malignant boredom and retirement neurosis.

The practical wisdom of Jesus knows no bounds. He is concerned with every aspect of our lives—from the cradle to the grave (and beyond). In this parable, Jesus is not scolding as much as he is making a plea. Here is a storyteller wisely warning ambitious entrepreneurs that a life of luxurious retirement, though earned and probably well-deserved, can also be nothing more than suffocating self-sufficiency.

Does this mean that there is something wrong with a luxury cruise or indulging a bit more in Agatha Christie? Hardly. Just as life can easily become excessively utilitarian—where everything done must have a purpose—it can equally become the opposite. As in most things, balance is the key.

The Bible has a great deal to say about weekends, vacations, sabbaticals, jubilees, and retirement, directly and by implication. For each one who works himself into the grave, there is one (or more) who loafs too much. Relaxation, changing the pace of our lives—enjoying a bicycle ride, or hauling in a marlin—is a tonic everyone needs, whether retired or just tired. Jesus is not saying in this parable that the farmer was a fool because he didn't want to work himself to death. He said he was a fool because he thought he could take care of himself—by himself—both before and after retirement.

It is not accidental or incidental that Jesus used the imagery of a farmer who built a bigger barn rather than a banker who built a bigger bank. The banker must depend on his expertise, while the farmer also depends on the weather. The point is that no man, entirely on his own, can succeed to the point that he has to build bigger barns or better banks. This is the folly to which Jesus is speaking. A man is a fool, says Jesus, who thinks otherwise.

Money and security, luxury and pleasure are not the ultimates in life. Nor can they be self-guaranteed. The farmer was a fool, not because he was trying to guard against his future, but because he thought he could guarantee it himself.

He was also a fool in that he was overly preoccupied with his own needs and wants, a malady which affects the rich as well as the poor. Jesus spoke of this with more imagery: "Look at the birds of the air and the flowers of the field. Doesn't God take care of their needs? Don't be overly anxious about today or tomorrow because you can't control the weather or the currency or even the number of your days" (see Matthew 5:25-34).

The rich farmer was also a fool in that he might have been more thoughtless than selfish. As far as it can be ascertained, he made no provision for sharing his blessings with others or protecting it from falling into wrong hands in the event something happened to him before he could spend his fortune. However, to his credit it should be stated that existing laws of inheritance probably obscured his need for any special provision unless he wanted to further safeguard his fortune or designate its surplus. It is to this point that attention should be given.

Perhaps you remember the little ditty which goes something like this:

Do your giving while you're living,
Then you'll be knowing where it's going.

Pretty sound advice. He was a fool, not only because he might not be around to spend what he had saved, but because he had missed the thrill of divvying it up—at least on paper—among family and friends, the disadvantaged and disabled.

Although it may be stretching the point a little to talk about the creation of a will in this context, it is implied. How many noble fortunes—great and small—fall into ignoble hands only God knows, and it must grieve him deeply.

No wonder Jesus called the rich man a fool. He wasn't asking the prosperous farmer to turn everything over to charity, thereby becoming a charity case himself. Rather, Jesus was cautioning him against the unenviable, pitiful plight of being the richest man in the cemetery—as well as the sad situation of existing insufferably, even in luxury, with full barns but an empty soul.

Rarely did Jesus give names to personalities in his

parables. In the second parable (Luke 16:19-31), there is a beggar by the name of Lazarus, which means "God has helped," a most fitting name. The rich man, the villain of the story, is unnamed (however, many commentators have named him Dives which in Latin means "rich").

Ironically, this rich man had reached the stage in life that was never quite reached in the previous parable. This man was retired (or at least had plenty of leisure) and lived in dazzling luxury. He dressed in the finest clothes that money could buy and feasted sumptuously day after day. But he too was a fool—another rich fool!

How then was this man a fool? Quite unlike the ill-advised farmer? In some ways yes. He was content to splurge his wealth on himself rather than salt away more. He was a big spender and seemingly was willing to diminish his wealth as he impoverished his soul.

It has already been established that people are entitled to an earned, well-deserved retirement; and it also has been established that there is no real virtue in piously relinquishing a fortune, thereby becoming a ward of the state or a burden to some reluctant relative. Few would be unwilling to grant this rich man three square meals a day plus a couple of coffee breaks, and even a midnight snack. But many would deny him the right to gorge himself day after day even if there were no beggar outside the gate going hungry or starving to death.

But outside the gate which guarded the estate of Dives lay Lazarus, a pathetic sight. This beggar, unable to walk, had to be brought daily to his begging corner where he lay, yearning for a crumb of bread or an understanding nod. From Dives he got neither.

There was no way the rich man could not know that Lazarus was there. In fact, it was probably a source of irritation to him that he lay there, and considerable annoyance that there were those who brought him there.

This, however, is the point Jesus wanted to make: Dives had no excuse. He was not oblivious to the world around him. Not only did he know Lazarus was there; in his comings and goings he nearly tripped over him. Although generally "ignorance is no excuse," Jesus was taking no chances as he planted Lazarus in his parable right at the gate rather than down the street or up an obscure alley. Dives was a fool because he almost had to fall on his face trying to avoid Lazarus.

Furthermore Jesus, although hardly exaggerating the scene (this was and is all too common), made Lazarus a hopeless, pathetic, tragic case. To stir our emotions? Perhaps, since this is often what it takes before we will lift a hand, but there is another reason.

We live in a world of cheap impostors, counterfeits, and lazy bums. There are those who seem to be miserable, poor, pathetic derelicts but are nothing more than clever freeloaders or polished panhandlers. They bend the laws and rip off the state. They work hard to avoid working and in short divert attention from those with legitimate needs. They hit and run as con artists, fake blindness, and masquerade as destitute spinoffs from a heartless society.

Jesus, who is hardly naive, portrays Lazarus, not as a wanton wastrel, but as a genuine down-and-outer. He was destitute, wracked with pain from his sore-covered body, nursed by stray dogs, and delivered to his begging post daily because he could not walk, much less run—or work. Dives could be excused for ignoring Lazarus if the poor beggar were simply too lazy to check the want ads or too rebellious to go along with the system. But Lazarus represents the legitimate poor, the helpless and homeless, the disabled and disadvantaged—and Dives did nothing about it. No wonder he was a fool.

Why didn't he do anything? Perhaps he was too occupied with his comfortable existence. He lived behind walls, sheltered from the ugly realities of life. He was, in fact, an oasis in a desert of poverty. Perhaps he was afraid that if he offered a cup of cold water his well might go dry. If he cared for Lazarus, he may have reasoned, another simply would take his place. He would run out of money before he could help everyone who needed it.

Perhaps he had built up an immunity to poverty and suffering. After all, Lazarus came daily, possibly year after

year. After awhile Dives would hardly know he existed.
He would see him, yet he wouldn't. It is tragic, but true,
that people can become oblivious to suffering and poverty,
sickness and even death. Jesus did his best to dramatize
the plight of Lazarus in order to jar the complacency of
his audience. It is possible to become anesthetized to the
human predicament.

Perhaps Dives felt that the responsibility for the care of
Lazarus lay elsewhere. He could have easily reasoned that
Lazarus needed the care of a physician, that he personally
could do little or nothing for the pathetic beggar who
obviously needed medical attention. It's possible that
Dives reasoned that he paid taxes and gave alms for such
situations. Consequently, others were more qualified—and
more responsible—to meet the multiple needs of Lazarus.

It's possible that the family (and friends) of Dives would
have objected if he gave a helping hand (this cannot be
overlooked). Even the amazing good Samaritan, he could
argue, brought the victim to an inn and not to his own
home (which of course is dangerously begging the
question).

Regardless of the reasons and rationalizations lurking
within the mind of Dives, he managed somehow to persist
throughout his luxurious existence until his death,
seemingly without any serious qualms or sleepless nights.

The plot thickens. Lazarus died, and although his body
was probably unceremoniously dragged to the city dump
(this was customary in those times), his soul did infinitely
better.

Dives also died. Both men became residents of an
eternal, rather mysterious abode of the dead which was
divided into two unbridgeable estates.

During the time of Jesus, rumors and speculation about
life after death were not uncommon. In fact, the Jews were
divided on the issue. The Sadducees, a onetime influential
group of religious aristocrats, often disputed with the
Pharisees about life after death. The Sadducees refused to
believe in any celestial sanctuary and were more than
displeased when Jesus told this parable.

It could be that Jesus had this in mind as he conceived this story. Although this parable is not a homily on eschatology, it did jolt the doubting Sadducees then just as it now plagues the annihilists (those who believe that the soul, especially of the unrepentant, dies with the body) and the transmigrationists (those who believe that at death the soul is transferred to another body).

Jesus was surrounded with eschatological folklore. There were many speculations and concepts about life and death, heaven and hell, Sheol and Gehenna, to say nothing about mortal and immortal deities.

Some say that Jesus borrowed a familiar Egyptian folk story as the basis for his parable. Others (and this is more likely) believe Jesus was refuting it. In either case, life after death was a live issue then as it always has been.

In this particular Egyptian folktale, a certain high priest was said to have overheard some loud laments. Looking down from his palatial balcony, he saw a rich man ceremoniously being transported to his resting place. Then he saw another procession. Here he witnessed a poor man, without any ceremony or lamenting, being taken to the burial field.

Later the high priest is taken to the abode of the dead. There they walk through several halls until they come to the seventh where he has the opportunity to witness an unusual scene. It seems that the bad deeds of the affluent man outweighed his good. Since the reverse was true of the poor man, they were required to exchange places in the abode of the dead.

The two stories are similar but hardly identical.

By depicting Lazarus in a comfortable, Eastern repose with a recognizable Abraham, and Dives in a most miserable position, Jesus was establishing an unmistakable point: after death, not everyone goes to the same place. There is more to life than a few short years followed by death; death becomes the key which unlocks the next gate.

More than that, Jesus pulled back the cloak of mystery surrounding the place called Hades. Until then, perhaps,

the Hebrews—divided as they were—thought of Hades as
an ethereal, wispy, shadowy place where recognition was
unlikely, probably even impossible. Dives recognized
Abraham whom he had never seen. Obviously we don't
have full understanding of all this.

Although it is impossible to create a doctrine of final
matters on the basis of this context, it can be suggested
that Jesus dramatized the parable sufficiently to say that
all roads do not lead to God or his paradise.

Lazarus and Dives, so close but so far apart in life,
found themselves so far apart, yet so close in death. Since
there is no indication, not even a suggestion, that Lazarus
had somehow outworked Dives in earning celestial points
while on earth, he must have gotten where he did in
another way.

There is good news in that no one can work himself
either into or out of heaven (or Hades). It is not what we
do, but what has been done for us that matters.

When the rich man discovered his predicament, he
tried to do something about it. As a rich man, Dives was
probably used to barking orders. Therefore, in the next
life he did the same (seemingly, people do not change
much over there). He asked Abraham to ask Lazarus (was
it below his dignity to speak directly to the former
beggar?) to get up (previously he couldn't walk), find
some water, dip his finger into it, and then go over the
great gulf to cool Dives' tongue. Actually he wasn't asking
for much, not even a cup of cold water.

Then again, Dives was asking for the impossible.
Abraham told him that the gulf was impossible to bridge.
It was then that Dives shifted from his own predicament
to that of his unrepentant brothers who were still living
(luxuriously it can be assumed). Thinking that a
messenger from the dead would be quite convincing,
Dives asked Abraham to ask Lazarus if he would go warn
his brothers.

Abraham wisely told him that if they wouldn't listen to
the law and the prophets, they wouldn't listen to a man
returned from the dead either.

For a moment, try to imagine that Lazarus was able to make a short journey back to earth. Try to visualize the scene. Lazarus, clad in new garments of obvious distinction—with no more sores covering his body—walks crisply to the gate of Dives' estate. After announcing his intention, what would happen?

The gatekeeper, recognizing Lazarus, might flee in fear, leaving the gate unattended. Or he could turn Lazarus in as an impostor. It is conceivable that Lazarus might be detained by his old friends or even run out of town. It is quite possible that he would have to get a health certificate from the local priest or a clean bill of health from the local psychiatrist. After all, it isn't every day that a man claims to have returned from the dead. He might find it most difficult to even get near the five brothers, much less have an audience with them.

But this is not the real problem. Even if Lazarus had made contact with the five, would they have listened? If they would have listened, would they have heeded the warning? Abraham said they wouldn't, and no doubt he is right. Jesus is warning against counting on a dramatic rescue from the wrong side of Hades, and he is telling us in his own way not to count on trauma to jolt us from our self-centered complacency. Foxhole conversions do exist, but they are highly unreliable.

Not much later—the echo of these words had hardly died away—the disciples found it difficult to believe that Jesus had risen from the dead just as he had said he would. Jesus did not count on his resurrection to greatly dramatize his mission. If anything, Jesus made his visible return to earth from the abode of the dead a low-key affair. Could it be that this parable is teaching that traumatic interventions are not a part of the eternal plan (it must be remembered that he refused to make a spectacular leap from the pinnacle of the Temple because it would smack of mere sensationalism)? Could it be, too, that Jesus is telling his listeners that time ran out for both Lazarus and Dives—and that it will run out for everyone, sooner or later? And that there are no second chances?

The Rich Fools

In the Egyptian folktale, the rich man was forced to exchange places with the poor man because of the imbalance in his good deed ledger. This is precisely what Jesus was not saying. The good news is that our position in the world to come is not based on a system of merit.

Nor is it even a meritocracy (a form of government run by persons in leading positions because of their ability, real or apparent).

In these parables about fools—fools for various reasons —it becomes apparent that God has a better idea. In fact, it could be put this way: God is no fool, nor is he fooled. We may have to wait until the life to come before God will prove his point, but he guarantees to do so. This is another part of the Good News.

CHAPTER NINE
MY FAIR LADIES
Matthew 25:1-13

This is a parable about five young ladies who didn't get to the wedding on time. They had undoubtedly dreamed about this exciting event and had every intention to be there. But at the last moment their heart's desire slipped through their fingers.

The pathos of this story is felt very deeply, not only by those who read about it today, but by the One who told it in the first place.

Jesus was coming down the homestretch of his earthly ministry. With death staring him in the face, what did he do? He told a charming oriental wedding story which ended unhappily.

Jesus was obviously heavy-hearted and must have felt a gnawing frustration. He had come to his own who treated him with anything from delight to disdain, mostly disdain. His own people generally rejected him, and the intimate few who followed him closely were about to scatter to the winds. Even Peter, the tough, aggressive, sometimes boisterous fisherman, wilted during the heat. Besides, going to the cross was not pleasant for Jesus. Being human as he was, it was not easy to surrender life's most precious gift, life itself. In addition, Jesus had to take upon his back the curse of mankind—sin. And although he turned the anathema of his cruel execution into a magnificent blessing, gloom hung heavily over him.

In the midst of this impending doom, Jesus warned those about him about that awful coming day when the door will be shut and bolted for the last time. But what a marvelous way he did it. Although the message was one of warning, the emphasis was on the celebration. Don't miss it, he urged.

Everyone loves a wedding (or almost everybody). With this in mind, Jesus told a plaintive, charming story about an ancient (for us) wedding. Although we never do get into the wedding itself, we share in its anticipation and advance preparations. As tour agencies say, planning a trip is half the fun. Though some might say that eloping is exciting, who could deny that planning a wedding is at least half the fun.

It is quite possible that Jesus had witnessed a situation like the one he described; thus the intensely personal nature of this parable. Whatever, there is such an intimacy that we both empathize and sympathize with the five luckless lassies.

It was a folk wedding, quite unlike the wedding given for the king's son which is discussed in the next chapter. If the bridal couple lived near but on opposite sides of a rural village, it was about an hour's distance from each other's parental homes. Often they had met in the village and had taken a strong liking to each other.

But alas, their parents did the courting in those days, and our young people could only hope and pray (and perhaps maneuver a little). The respective families agreed that this would be an excellent match, and negotiations were begun to make the necessary arrangements for the engagement. The engagement was announced, perhaps a year in advance, depending upon the age of the youth and other criteria.

Now the time for the wedding had arrived, but there was one more last-minute detail to arrange: the respective fathers had to make the final marital negotiations. During the engagement period, certain conditions could have changed, slightly or more dramatically, and it was essential that the respective fathers (and even other family members) discuss (or argue) in order to satisfy the demands placed upon them. It could have been a stubborn dowry question, or newly developed suspicions relative to the groom's ability to provide for his bride in the best possible manner. In some instances, these negotiations could take hours, or even days, thereby delaying the actual wedding.

Sooner or later the haggling would be resolved, and the groom, together with his friends, would form a procession which took him to the home of the bride where she would join him, together with her friends, in the pilgrimage back to his parental home where the wedding would take place.

In this particular case, the procession did not depart until late at night, necessitating torches which created a rather dramatic scene. The bride, waiting in her parental home, would be on the lookout for her bridegroom. Occasionally torch-lit parades would appear; the word would go out that he was coming, only to bring disappointment because it was another procession which turned off in another direction.

More watching, and possibly more disappointments, came. At first it was easy to keep the festive mood going because the expectation was high. As the hours slipped by, the bridesmaids, wisely, elected to catch a few winks. After all, a couple of hours spent dozing could come in mighty handy toward dawn when the celebration would be picking up momentum.

Finally the long awaited shout came, and this time it

was the groom. The ten bridesmaids quickly awakened, trimmed their torches (in all probability this is what was meant by lamps), and readied themselves for the procession. Unfortunately, five of the ten girls had not taken any extra oil with them. Since they had already used up all or most of their oil, they asked the five wise maidens if they could have some of theirs. After all, they were good friends, weren't they?

Knowing that if they shared their oil all ten of them would run out, the wise five refused, suggesting that the others quickly run and get their own. But at midnight?

In panic and near tears, the girls ran off to the nearest merchant who naturally was asleep. By the time they arrested his attention, pleaded their case, and persuaded him to sell them the necessary oil, valuable time was wasted. Finally they had their precious oil and hurried off to catch the procession, which unfortunately they never caught.

Why, we ask, couldn't they march in the procession without a torch? Certainly there would be plenty of light and after all, who would notice? This is logical reasoning, and acceptable perhaps for the West in the twentieth century. But not for first-century Palestine. Tradition, and perhaps even law, made it both improper and impossible for a young maiden to be out after dark without her own torch. To everyone in the wedding party, it was unthinkable to march in the procession without a torch. There was no way they could "hitchhike" on the torch of another, and they knew it. But why were they unprepared?

That is the question of the hour! If they knew that the procession might be delayed until the dark hours of midnight . . . if they knew they would probably need extra oil . . . if they saw that the other five had extra oil with them, how could they be so negligent? We don't know.

In those days when the door was closed to the wedding guests, it was bolted from the inside and no one— meaning *no one*—was admitted. The door remained locked, even though the bride knew her bridesmaids would soon be coming. Even she could not open the door. Jesus knew this when he told this parable, and we too must understand it or we cannot grasp the significance of the story.

What a pitiful, pathetic sight. Five close friends of the bride were on the outside looking in. They could pound on the door, throw pebbles at the shutters, yell and scream, weep, and even throw tantrums—but nothing could or would open the door. There they stood, five beautiful tear-stained damsels—so near, yet so far away.

We of the twentieth century find this difficult to comprehend. When my wife and I were married, some dear friends of ours drove from Minnesota to Michigan where the wedding took place. But they arrived after the ceremony because they had failed to take into account the time difference between the two states. Although we were saddened that they had missed the ceremony, we were delighted that they could participate in the reception. It would have been unthinkable, even unpardonable, for us to have excluded them because they arrived late.

This is why we find this parable so disconcerting. No doubt there were valid reasons why the door was bolted shut and equally valid reasons why the bolting of the door had become such an inviolable tradition as well as a necessary precaution. We could argue relentlessly that the young ladies were entitled to be admitted under the circumstances, but it would not have availed two thousand years ago.

The point Jesus was making had nothing to do with the tradition of bolted doors at wedding feasts. He was simply but effectively saying that some people who are expected to be there, who seem entitled to participate, and who had fully intended to be there won't be there.

These young women under the circumstances made a heroic effort to get there. They were not bad girls. To the contrary, they were probably the finest in the land. But they were unprepared. Were they careless, indifferent, lackadaisical, procrastinators, or simply oblivious to reality? Perhaps they had gotten by before and simply assumed the other girls would share their oil with them. Maybe they were scatterbrained or rattle-headed. Maybe they just liked to live dangerously. Whatever, they knew the rules and were reminded of them as they saw the extra oil carried by the wiser of the ten.

The wise maidens should also be given a word of commendation. Perhaps two. They knew that if they shared their oil, there might be ten on the outside rather than five. Besides, although the distinction is often blurred, there is a keen difference between magnanimity and reckless generosity. Although it is quite possible for one to lay down one's life for another, that is not the message Jesus was unfolding in this story. One, or all five, could have given their oil to the thoughtless maidens, but that is not the issue. The message is rather indelible that one cannot travel on the grace of another. Each of the girls was on her own.

The five, in addition to missing the wedding, must have been further disappointed in the anguish they caused their dearest friend, the bride. Even though the celebration continued possibly until the wee hours of the morning, and possibly longer (some weddings lasted days), some of the joy doubtless was missing because some expected guests were not there.

The point Jesus was making comes alive when the facts are known. If, however, we read too much into the parable, it quickly becomes an allegory and the message becomes obscure. One must then scurry about to ascertain meanings for each aspect of the story such as the oil, the lamps, the significance of the number ten (and five), the midnight hour, the bolted door, the bride and the groom, and even the road on which they traveled.

Although there are secondary overtones as there are in most of the parables, this is not an allegory, and hardly an allegorical parable. The meaning is quite simple, direct, and universal: many who fully intend to attend the Eternal Wedding Celebration will not quite make it. Nor will there be a second chance. Living dangerously is just that—dangerous.

CHAPTER TEN
**THE GUEST WITHOUT
A WEDDING ROBE**
Matthew 22:1-14

One is tempted to subtitle this parable "There's One in Every Crowd." But that is deceptive because it goes much deeper than that.

In the last chapter we witnessed a folk wedding, although we actually never quite made it into the ceremony or joined in the festive celebration which followed. In this wedding story, the whole social milieu is different. Or at least it was intended to be that way.

It might be even more difficult to reconstruct a typical royal wedding of long ago than a folk celebration. Besides, it is perhaps equally difficult not to think Western as we attempt to visualize an Eastern wedding. But even though there is disagreement as well as lack of evidence, we shall attempt to think Eastern—ancient Eastern, that is.

The marriage of a king's son would be considerably different than the marriage of a carpenter's daughter or a cobbler's son. This marriage would be a royal, festive occasion, possibly a medley of overtones of political intrigue and high-society one-upmanship. Invitations would be issued long before the event with RSVP deeply engraved. Once the invitation was acknowledged, it was a grievous breach of etiquette to renege. But that is exactly what happened.

The king sent his servants to summon those who had previously been invited, but the servants were rebuffed. The king, mystified and angered, sent other servants (perhaps more persuasive) to inform the invited guests that the wedding feast would soon begin. In fact, the ox was already turning on the spit. Everything was ready.

The guests not only jested and turned their backs on the king's messengers, they manhandled some of them, even killing not a few. Such gratitude!

By this time, Jesus no doubt had his listeners' full attention. They probably had never heard of such audacity and wondered what on earth Jesus could be driving at. They soon found out, but not before Jesus told about the king exploding in anger as he sent his troops to retaliate by killing the murderers and burning their city. The simple little wedding story was turning out to be quite a tale, but it wasn't over yet.

Now the king did another unpredictable thing: he sent other servants to go out and invite anyone and everyone to the wedding feast. This they did, and before long the king's court was filled with all kinds of people, bad and good.

Word was sent to the king that the guests had arrived, and the king came to greet them in person. Again, imagination must be employed, but with calculated restraint.

As each guest arrived, from the streets and alleys, countryside and hilltops, most of them were over-whelmed by the grandeur and were, of course, unprepared. The servants, with the ox still rotating on

The Guest Without A Wedding Robe

the spit and very well-done by this time, urged the newly invited guests to make no delay. The word was clear: hurry, hurry, hurry. The people had no time to go home and freshen up, or to go to the nearest boutique.

However, as they arrived at the palace, they were admitted into the grand vestibule. There each guest was given the opportunity to freshen up a bit and don the wedding robe which the king had provided. Each guest, therefore, looked alike, and it was this robe which gained him entrance to the banquet hall where the feast would take place.

As the king descended down the elegant stairway to greet his guests, all dressed in dazzling white, he spotted one guest still in street clothes. Going directly to the man, the king asked him how he got in there without a wedding robe. The man was speechless. Without a further word, the king told his servants to throw him out, and out he went. And there the parable ends. Once again we are left at the entry to the celebration, and once again our imaginations are forced to work overtime.

Our family was privileged to live in Sweden in 1976 when the young bachelor king Carl XVI Gustaf married a charming young woman by the name of Sylvia. Naturally we were not invited. The kingly circuit was not the road on which the Seagrens traveled. However, there were invited guests, and most if not all of them came—in royal splendor. What a tragedy it would have been if the king had given Sweden a beautiful new queen but no one had bothered to witness the ceremony. In fact, the thought of such an occurrence boggles the mind. But that is what Jesus wanted to do. He wanted to boggle some minds.

To allegorically understand this parable, which seems to be both historical and prophetical, the elements must be kept under restraint. It is a parable, but not a simple one. The simple message would be that Jesus came unto his own, but his own received him not; but as many as received him, to them were given the right to attend the wedding feast. This message is clear. Those who were first invited made light of it, putting their jobs and daily matters first, or even acting indecently. However, the invitation went out again. This time it was unrestricted.

Now, we must allow some elbow room in the interpretation, but not too much. It does appear that the king's son typifies Jesus, and that would make the king represent God. The invited, responding guests would be those who heard the message and responded, and all except one was admitted to the wedding feast where the bride (the company of believers, also known as the Church) would be joined to the groom (Christ who claimed his bride). The servants who extended the original invitation would be the prophets (and others) of old who proclaimed God's message to a select nation. The later servants could represent the apostles who would be ignored, shamefully treated, and even martyred.

But now the parable becomes prophetic rather than historical. To piece together each parcel of the parable into a tidy message is almost impossible, but it is extremely tempting. This is especially true if we think of the king as a prototype of Jehovah God. Jesus never did say that the king was God or that he was the son about to be married. But we do. Yet when we do, God becomes a deity of rage and revenge rather than joy. Has God destroyed a city of inhabitants out of revenge because apostles or missionaries or prophets were ignored or despised? Maybe. Maybe not.

We do know, however, that God has taken swift action against a city which had reached the absolute bottom of human degradation (Sodom) and temporarily reprieved another (Nineveh) when it repented. In this parable, there is no indication that the king gave the ungrateful jesters or the intolerant murderers anything but revenge as he sent his troops to destroy and burn. This kind of behavior is historically accurate. The listeners knew about kings who could and would take revenge. That was a part of the shock treatment, but it is not a description of God in parabolic form. This is why, even though we can and do see patterns of complicated theology and prophecy coming through the parables, it is dangerous to stretch

The Guest Without
A Wedding Robe

parables into free-flowing and sometimes unending allegories.

Therefore, even though it is possible to read much more into this parable, perhaps, than it warrants, we will now go to the other extreme and attempt to read out of the parable some meaningful thoughts.

First, there is the matter of *priorities*.

Every generation believes (or wants to believe) that the good go eternally to a different place than the wicked, but not every generation knows where or why. In this parable, Jesus reminds his listeners that not only the brazen, defiant, evil, unregenerate, and unrepentant scoundrels will meet their doom in some awful place, but that those who are generally well thought of may meet the same fate.

Of those who were originally invited to the great wedding feast, according to the parable, not a single one attended, as far as is known. However, this may be reckless exegesis because the emphasis is not on a total rejection but on an indiscriminate repudiation. Those who refused to attend the wedding even though presumably they had acknowledged the invitation declined for various reasons.

Some simply refused. They would not come.

Others shrugged or laughed it off, going on with their ordinary routines of farming and merchandising. In other words, their regular concerns were more important to them than attending the wedding of their crown prince (assuming that this was the eldest son).

However, others were not content to shrug it off or make a joke of it. For some reason, they took the invitation as an insult or a threat, manhandling the messengers of the king, even killing some of them. This seems preposterous except that history verifies the shameful treatment of bearers of good news. There are martyrs, seemingly, in every age.

There is also a matter of *progression* here.

The first rejection was a simple "No thanks, not today." However, the next response was less polite. In fact, it was downright impolite as they made light of it. Their refusal to take it seriously resulted in their misallocation of priorities. They preferred to live for today (as most people do) as though there is no tomorrow. They were seemingly content to get bogged down in their everyday routine rather than interrupt it to celebrate with the king in his happiness.

Only when we get to the third reaction to the invitation do we come to those who most of the world would say deserved their fate. Because of their shameful behavior, people would reason, they deserved death. Most would agree to this in principle, but would balk if they thought Jesus was talking about eternal death. They, like the others, missed the wedding feast, not because they were turned away, but because they refused the invitation.

Jesus seems to be saying that there is eternal danger in misplaced priorities. The great wedding feast—symbolical certainly of eternal life with God and his Son—will be missed by the polite refusers, the nonchalant, even jesting regulars (the salt of any typical community), as well as defiant, brazen sinners. They will not be there, not because of what they have done, but because of what they didn't do. They didn't accept the invitation.

As Jesus told this parable, he knew that many who heard would fall into one of these categories and he wanted to jolt them out of their complacency, levity, or hostility. And he still does.

Next, there is the matter of *pretension*.

The wedding guests who came to the feast must have been a motley crew. How many, if any, of the originally invited came is not known. Even so, the mixture must have been something: rich man, poor man, beggar, thief. Undeserving, but all welcome.

Incredible as it may seem to many today, there are still those who believe they will be the only ones in heaven. The ancient Jews, who were known for their exclusive snobbishness when it came to religious rewards, were stunned by the audacity of Jesus who told this incredible story. No king in his right mind would do such a thing, they would reason. Heaven, if there is such a place, they would argue, is for us, not the riffraff of our society.

Later, the disciples of Jesus found it difficult to accept the fact that a person could indeed accept the invitation of God's grace without becoming a Jew first.

When Jesus told this story, he was making an incontestable case: the invitation was for everyone, anyone who would accept. With no exceptions. And they came, the good and the bad.

Why? For many reasons. They came because they were curious. They wanted to see the inner workings of the king's house. They came because the servants were persuasive. They came to get a free meal. They came because they felt sorry for the king when they heard what had happened. They came because they were social climbers. They came because there was nothing else exciting to do. They came because their friends were going. They came because they couldn't think of an excuse not to come.

But there were many who didn't come. It would be inconceivable to think of a palace with a banquet hall large enough for all the inhabitants of the kingdom, or even the royal city. No, only a fraction of those within hailing distance could be accommodated. Just how many of those who were invited rejected the invitation we cannot be sure, but we do know by past as well as present experience that most, unfortunately, excuse themselves.

However, one man came along with the others. He, too, was invited and came for some reason or other. In spite of the almost infinite variety of reasons and motivations which prompted the guests to respond initially, this man evidently was an impostor.

When the guests, who were freely invited with no strings attached, arrived, they were asked to don a wedding garment. They did, all except one. Reading between the lines, which we are forced to do at times, we can only make a calculated guess as to why he refused.

Was he simply a stubborn fool? Or was the robe the

wrong size or color? Was he a rugged individualist who insisted on doing things his own way? Perhaps he thought his own clothes were good enough, or better than the king's garment? Was he absent-minded, a procrastinator ("I fully intended to wear the robe, but I hadn't gotten around to it"), or what?

Because he was speechless when the king accosted him, we have reason to believe that he had no valid reason, not even a feeble excuse. Any of the above excuses might have been offered, but he ventured nothing. This, then, tends to incriminate him in two ways. Either he willfully refused to explain his behavior, or he couldn't. Had he said that he didn't know that he was supposed to wear a robe, he might have been given another chance. After all, he still was not actually in the banquet hall. Or if he would have asked the king's pardon for his thoughtlessness or stubborn pride or whatever, he might have had a last minute reprieve.

However, because he was a pretender, an impostor, he was unceremoniously ushered out and the banquet began —without him. Like the five young, unwise maidens, he was so close but missed the celebration.

There have been, and are, and will be many pretenders. Pretension is not a harmless little ploy. It is a dangerous game, and Jesus was warning the pretenders, the smug hypocrites, that their sins will find them out even though it might not be until the last second. The king was no fool. Neither is God.

Finally, there is the matter of *predestination*.

As mentioned earlier, the parables are a check and balance system which correct or explain doctrinal ambiguities. Predestination is certainly one of the biblical mysteries. Because is is taught in Scripture, we should probe into its implications. Taken out of its context, however, predestination becomes a brutal doctrine. It turns God into a kind of a celestial casino cardsharp who deals out the destinies of mankind: one for heaven, one for hell, one for purgatory, one for limbo ... and then proceeds to lose count. When taken in its extreme form, predestination becomes an evil which renders the will ineffective and becomes mere fatalism: what is meant to be will be and I can do nothing about it.

This parable shatters this absurd handling of a delicate subject, and reminds us dramatically that the invitation went out into every nook and cranny of the community. The servants did not force any of the prospective guests to go to the feast. They did not club them into submission or ply them with tangibles or intangibles. They did not warn them of the consequences if they didn't taste the food the king had prepared. They simply invited, pleaded, and persuaded, and made everyone within range feel welcome. But the people had to decide whether or not they would attend.

There is a mysterious relationship between the wooing unto himself by the heavenly Father and the response to this wooing. No guest could go to the wedding feast without being invited, and no person can determine his own salvation any old time he pleases. The invitation may be repeated (the servants perhaps went up and down the same roadway more than once) or it may be given once. The crucial fact is this: when the invitation is given, what will we do with it? This is the mysterious duality of the gospel. As a matter for the record, many are called but few respond. Put another way, many are invited but few choose to attend.

Tragic, but true.

CHAPTER ELEVEN
**THE SHEEP
AND THE GOATS**
Matthew 25:31-46

While traveling in Turkey (a part of biblical Syria) a
number of years ago, I took a picture of a typical
shepherd with his flock. After showing the slide a number
of times, I was chagrined when it finally dawned on
me that the sheep were actually goats.

At a distance they can look identical, and often sheep
and goats will be tended by the same guardian. After
making this embarrassing discovery, the disturbing
imagery Jesus used in this parable has taken on a much
more significant meaning.

Ewes and lambs can and do play innocently together.
But as they mature, it's quite a different story. Billy goats
can be mean customers, and we have learned not to
underestimate the power of a ram either. Besides,
mountain sheep can be equally surefooted as any goat.

Their similarities and dissimilarities are intriguing.

Before attributing too much allegorical value to the sheep and goat imagery, we ought to remind ourselves that even though our sins can be made as white as wool and there are black sheep in many families, nothing is said whether the sheep were white and goats black—or if they were mixed in color. What must be remembered is that the sheep were separated from the goats, not the white sheep from the black goats, or the black sheep from the white and then from the goats.

At night, a good shepherd would often separate the sheep (who liked the cool invigorating night air) from the goats (who preferred the warmth of a cave). But this is not the separation Jesus is talking about. He is talking about the final separation—the separation in which the sheep and goats part ways forever.

When that day comes, make no mistake. The shepherd is unlike the naive tourist photographer who didn't know the difference between a sheep and a goat.

The parable of the ten young maidens reminded us that the day Jesus was talking about could be temporarily delayed.

The parable of the man without a wedding garment prepared the mind for the sobering fact that impostors may almost, but not quite, crash the party.

Now Jesus was ready to inform his listeners—friend and foe alike—that this day of expectation would indeed arrive. To the Jews, it meant the end of a rather rotten world and the ushering in of a marvelous era of peace and prosperity, with God triumphing over every visible and invisible enemy.

To the believers, it meant the end of the tyranny of sin and evil, sham and hypocrisy—a new heaven and a new earth, with the world of evil conquered and destroyed—a place where tears will be wiped away, forever.

Actually, the two positions were similar in many ways, and Jesus had ready listeners when he talked of the separation of the wicked from the good. The critical problem facing them was not that it wouldn't be done,

but how? Who are the good guys and who are the bad
guys? How can the one be differentiated from the other—
at least in borderline cases?

The listeners were pretty much agreed that Jesus was
talking about a fulfillment of the ancient promises—
that godlessness would come to a grinding halt, justice
and judgment would emerge victorious, and for the Jews,
the long awaited Messiah would be revealed in all his
glory. But for the Christians, their hope was that their
Messiah, who had already come, would finally be
vindicated and accepted as the true Messiah by everyone.

In order to gain insight into the judgment scenario,
three parables ought to be examined together. We must
remember, however, that scholars are not agreed on when
and where Jesus told his parables. Entire doctoral
dissertations have been devoted to such subjects as the
editing process of Saint Matthew and Doctor Luke. This
juxtaposition doubtless will raise some questioning,
particularly because Matthew pushed them twelve
chapters apart. But it must be remembered as well that
many of the parables are not limited to one topic, and
that even though they may not be siblings, they certainly
could be at least first cousins.

Before going on into the discussion of the sheep and
the goats, the wheat and the weeds, and the net and the
fish, another parable previously mentioned ought to be
brought out of retirement.

Because the parable of the leaven (Matthew 13:33) is so
often misunderstood, it might be well to remind ourselves
that the leavening process is one of mysterious intrigue
whereby a tiny bit of yeast can permeate a huge lump
of dough (within reason) until the whole mass is affected.
It is this process that is continually going on in the
Kingdom; but on the other hand, a tiny bit of yeast
struggling against a ton of dough could be said to be
waging a losing battle.

The implication of the parable about the yeast was that
a handful of yeasty Christians permeate an evil society,
transforming it into something better. Leaven should not

be thought of as something evil. But on the other hand, leaven can be evil, and unrighteousness can and does spread throughout society as well. Therefore, in every kingdom there are forces of good and evil struggling against the odds, and every society—including the Kingdom of God—is a curious blend of good and evil, righteousness and unrighteousness, believers and nonbelievers. But more than that, it is also a mixture of counterfeits, hypocrites, do-gooders, and no-gooders who live side by side. Unfortunately, as time went on, the leavening of good seems to have been overwhelmed by the leaven of evil, resulting in an unbelievably complicated society.

The world, the Kingdom of God, and Christendom are incredible conglomerations of saints and sinners, so hopelessly entwined that only the Son of man and his angels can do the job of eventually disentangling society.

Thank God for that!

THE SHEEP AND THE GOATS (Matthew 25:31-46)

For those whose philosophy is "eat, drink, and be merry for tomorrow we die," the idea of a final judgment is terribly disconcerting and dismissed, if possible, as mere myth.

But Matthew took Jesus seriously and made a rather awesome case for a final judgment, not only of individuals but of nations. To some, it was exceedingly good news to know that the wicked will not get away with their mischief, individually or collectively. For others, it was more comforting to realize that righteousness would not go unnoticed.

If one is not careful, this passage could easily be misunderstood. Although it talks about feeding the poor and nursing the ill, nowhere does it suggest that those who feed the hungry or nurse the ill will be exonerated for their evil deeds. The sheep and the goats were separated before Jesus questioned them. The question of righteousness and unrighteousness had already been established.

The next stage, then, sees Jesus questioning them about the leavening influence of their respective righteousness and unrighteousness.

In other words, the Judge is not only concerned with the credentials of the sheep and goats; he wants to know about their productivity as well. The godly were responsible for leavening their society for good; the ungodly were responsible for the fact that they had made society a worse place in which to live.

When questioned, the righteous had a comeback: they had fed the hungry and visited prisoners. But the unrighteous had no comeback. Their plunge into the eternal fire was not because they failed to feed the poor and clothe the naked. They were doomed because they were ungodly, and because they were ungodly they did not enrich the world in which they lived. God is no fool, and what a man sows he shall reap. The ungodly do not improve the world.

Rarely did Jesus state or imply directly that he was a central figure in any of his parables. However, in this case, there is hardly a doubt that Jesus Christ, the Son of man, is God's deputy judge. There is no other viable alternative.

In this sense, it is a good thing that the carpenter from Nazareth, who also knew sheep from goats, is doing the judging rather than a naive, city-slicker pilgrim-photographer.

THE WHEAT AND THE WEEDS (Matthew 13:24-30, 36-43)

We have just seen that the Son of man will be the ultimate supreme judge, separating the righteous from the unrighteous with uncanny accuracy and compassion. In this parable we get another picture, not contradictory but complementary.

A farmer had sown the best seed possible, probably selected from a previous harvest. While waiting for the day of harvest, his hired men noticed something strange. Rather than the usual amount of weeds cropping up, the whole field seemed to be infected. Someone who disliked the owner—or even hated him—had shrewdly sown the obnoxious weed during the middle of the night. Undetected, because darnel (a weedy grass) and wheat look alike during the first part of the growing season, the bastard wheat (as darnel is sometimes called) got a good start.

Wisely, the owner told his men to let the wheat and weeds grow together, lest in pulling up the weeds the wheat would also be uprooted. It is at this point extremely important to note that the owner was not protecting the make-believe wheat; he was safeguarding his crop.

Later he gave instructions to harvest the entire crop, weeds and all, but to put the darnel into bundles, presumably for kindling—a prudent move, especially in a land where firewood was scarce.

In the separation of the sheep from the goats, we have a clear distinction between two differing species. In the separation of the false from the genuine wheat, the distinction is not as clear.

At one time, darnel had been genuine wheat, but it had dissipated itself until it degenerated into a pesky, worthless substance. However, it was in the same grain family, and in its earliest stages no one except an expert could tell the difference, not even upon close examination. But, as the "fruit" began to appear, the difference became telling until it was obvious, even to nonexperts. The picture we see is this: the spurious wheat is growing together with the genuine wheat, enjoying the same soil, moisture, and sun—until the harvest.

Anyone involved in the work of the Kingdom of God (or in various Christian circles) sooner or later—too often later—discovers that there are spurious and genuine believers living and working together, often in close harmony. Some of the hypocrites or pretenders are hiding in the woodwork, but others live openly. Pastors and bishops, committees and boards have been fooled countless times, and they too have been guilty of insincerity. At times the church simply winks at a phony rather than create a fuss—sometimes a wise act but at times a cowardly deed.

Just as a king is confronted with plaguing problems in knowing what to do with disloyal subjects, so it is in Christendom. What should be done with heretics and hypocrites, pious phonies and pedigreed pew-sitters? Should they be ignored or burned at the stake? Should they be publicly whipped or simply excommunicated? Should they be shunned or admonished? Or should they be left alone in the hopes they will repent or disappear, or at least lose their effectiveness?

Jesus clearly warned that the Kingdom of God being established on earth would not be heavenly. He warned that the church would have its enemies, and one major enemy whom Jesus mentions specifically. The devil is a wily creature, ignored by many, relegated to the Middle Ages and beyond by others, and underestimated by nearly everyone. This shrewd manipulator, this ingenious, diabolical adversary discovered that one of the most effective ways to sabotage the Kingdom of God was to infiltrate it.

We chuckle at the fading adage, "The devil made me do it," but he does too often have the upper hand. The whole realm of Christendom is riddled with darnel: hypocrites, impostors, saboteurs, phonies, and dupes. These, and others, are aided by the superficial, insincere, naive, gullible, lazy, and worldly-minded.

Jesus makes it very clear: citizens of the Kingdom of God are finite. To disentangle the genuine from the spurious takes infinite wisdom. God has chosen to allow believers and nonbelievers as well as the spurious to live together until the Judge, in his infinite wisdom, separates the godly from the ungodly, the pretenders from the genuine.

But does this mean that there should be no church discipline of any kind? Hardly. Our ecclesiastical forefathers have all struggled with this malady, and the battle goes on. Rather recently a prominent bishop was charged with heresy, among other accusations, but the ecclesiastical structure was so constituted that a trial (much less a conviction) was virtually impossible. On the other hand, others have been defrocked simply for stumbling in the Lord's Prayer or chanting off-key.

Church discipline and order in the Kingdom is a crucial matter. Although the parable does seem to suggest that tolerance is mandatory, patience might be a better word. In no way can it be said that the parable is defending the spurious citizens of the Kingdom. Contrarily, it is the genuine that are being protected. If rooting out the hypocritical tares will injure the growth of the wheat, it is best to let them grow together.

But there is a risk. In the parable of the sower, the danger of the weeds overpowering and choking the good grain was pointed out. There may be times when it is imperative to remove the spurious—when possible and practical, that is. But in the parable of the wheat and the weeds, it was both impossible and impractical.

A practical solution, then, might be to exercise wise discernment as an assessment of a situation is made. Seed is sown, not indiscriminately but generously, and some will fall or will be blown into weedy soil. This is one of the risks that the sower must take, and he knows it.

Another risk is that someone will sabotage the field. This is quite another matter.

Consequently, in the day of judgment, the task of separating the wheat from the tares, and the wheat from the chaff, is not the task of the human sower. The responsibility and difficulty demand eternal wisdom and absolute justice that only the Son of man can give.

Within every church, denomination, and ecumenical body there are devout, godly, sincere, genuine believers intermingled with counterfeits, impostors, and misguided unbelievers. Somewhere between these lie the weak, the shallow, the indolent, opportunists, and the like. There are also hand-clappers, back-slappers, pious politicians (in the negative sense), and manipulators who somehow manage to land prestigious pulpits and sit at the fattest desks while countless godly, dedicated, hard-working, deserving stalwarts of the faith plod through ecclesiastical marshes, doomed as it were to rather insignificant posts and unprestigious parishes. Humanly speaking, justice is often nonexistent.

This parable reveals the awesome truth that God is neither fooled nor mocked, and will someday assess everyone—believer and nonbeliever. More than that, he will separate the ingenious pretenders, so often blessed with uncanny good fortune (or who are diabolically shrewd), from those who possess a genuine faith.

The one who sows the degenerate seed is inhuman. Therefore, it will take one who is superhuman to disentangle the harvest.

THE NET AND THE FISH (Matthew 13:47-50)

The previous parable said in effect: "You do the sowing, I'll do the reaping!" What a blessed relief, actually, that believers do not have to stand in judgment of their fellow human beings. This is neither a prerogative nor a privilege. What an awesome, terrifying thing it would be to put the destiny of the human race into finite hands. The famous (or to some, infamous) sermon preached by Jonathan Edwards, "Sinners in the Hands of an Angry God," would almost be equaled or excelled by a sermon preached on "Sinners in the Hands of Angry Saints."

In this third parable of the trilogy, we discover another dimension. A net was either dragged ashore between two fishing boats or hauled in by long lines. As the net swept the sea, anything in the way would be caught and hauled ashore. It has been said that the Sea of Galilee, where no doubt this parabolic imagery was drawn, contains over twenty species of fish, including the delicious Peter Fish still enjoyed by residents and tourists.

As the haul reaches shore, the fisherman examines each fish individually. Typically, the professional fisherman deliberately, painstakingly, and personally sorts out the miscellaneous catch, throwing out the debris and undesirable fish. It is a laborious but necessary process as he considers both dietary and ecological laws.

In this trilogy there are several common imageries. An important one is this: in no case is a careless, random, casual disposition allowable, whether you are involved with animal, grain, or fish.

There are significant differences as well. As the fisherman hauls in the net, unlike the sower he does not know what he will get. No doubt at times he is surprised, amused, or disappointed. Again, unlike the sower who settles down to await the harvest, the fisherman cleans his nets and sets out again.

The sower reaps what is sown, but the fisherman catches but a fraction of the fish in the sea. At times his net may be empty. Another time it may break because of too many fish. While it could be argued effectively that the parable is teaching the necessity of a continual sorting process (in contrast to letting the wheat and tares grow together), this is not the heart of the parable.

Among various ways of handling this story, this thought seems to emerge and should not be overlooked: the Kingdom of God is not unlimited either in size or influence, although it is large. Fishermen fish but do not exhaust the seas. Far from it (except for contemporary exploiters of fishing grounds).

Earlier it was mentioned that the influence of the Kingdom of Heaven extended considerably beyond its subjects and borders. The same is true of Christendom. Today, for instance, of the approximately four billion people on earth, almost one billion of them are considered Christian. Even so, there are still three billion "fish" swimming in the seas. Not all of them have been caught, nor will they be caught. And of the one billion, only God knows how many of them are genuine.

It seems, therefore, that this parable is trying to tell us that the Kingdom of Heaven will not embrace every member of every tribe and nation. As the fishers of men sweep the seas in search of fish, the majority of fish will not be caught. More fishermen are needed but will not be found.

Again, if the parable of the net and the fish were the only judgment parable, there might be difficulty in wondering about the fish which are never caught as well as the fish which are thrown away or tossed back into the waters. But when seen together, the picture is complete.

As believers, our task is to be faithful in tending the flock, in sowing the seed, in hauling in the net. We must realize that there will be goats mingling with sheep, tares among the wheat, and some fish will get away. But God knows this and has taken it into account in his own way.

Incredible as it may seem (but how true!), we cannot guarantee a good harvest any more than we can fill the net and empty the sea. There are matters pertaining to the Kingdom of God which lie beyond our grasp, and the judgment of our fellowmen is one of them.

One final word ought to be said. There is another common denominator inherent in each of these parables: judgment comes at the end of the age!

Yes, there are minor judgments and adjustments which must continually be made, but the ultimate judgment does not come during one's lifetime, nor at one's death. No person or nation can be equitably judged until all the evidence is in, and that will occur only when God, in his infinite wisdom, calls our era to a close.

At that time, and not before, the Son of man will be called upon to execute a fair, impartial, omniscient judgment of all mankind, believers and nonbelievers, which will result in an uncontested verdict. Why? Because it is going to be a divine, absolute, perfectly just judgment of reward and recognition, and of dealing out justice and banishment. Amen (so be it).

CHAPTER TWELVE
GOOD NEWS IS EXPENSIVE
Matthew 13:44-46

Since the picture of an ancient biblical kingdom framed
in many minds is so vague, think of a medieval castle,
moat and all. The castle, which doubles as a fortress, is a
formidable obstacle when the drawbridge is down and the
gates are slammed shut.

Entrance into this bastion is virtually impossible unless
the king decrees otherwise. Then the gates are swung
wide open, the bridge is lowered, and whosoever wills
may enter.

To many—too many—this is the picture of Christianity:
The gate is always open, night and day, and anyone who
desires to enter may do so—whenever it is convenient.
If there are more interesting things to do for awhile
outside, well and good—or if there are matters more
pressing than entering the domain of the king, then on

with them. One can always enter at an opportune moment. The gate, naturally, is open, the guard is away, and the drawbridge is always down.

Or is it?

These two parables probe deeply into the cost of Christianity. In short, they say that there is no such thing as cheap grace. They are dramatic reminders that Christianity is not an add-on religion. The Christian faith is not free. In fact, it is expensive, even for the rich, because it demands an equitable price: everything!

When a rich man hears about a great bargain, he says, "How much is it?" as he reaches for his wallet. The poor man sighs wistfully, mumbling, "If only I were a rich man."

Jesus was confronted with an incredible situation. Knowing that both rich and poor—and every shade between—would want to enter the Kingdom, he had to make sure that the entrance fees were equitable. In all probability there was no better way to illustrate this than to put it into a couple of ingenious parables.

We also know that the rich young ruler walked away, dejected, because the price he was asked to pay was too high: "Go, sell everything you have and give the money to the poor." He *couldn't* do that because he *wouldn't*. To the poor widow, with a couple of almost worthless mites clutched in her fist, the message was the same: "Give all of them!" And she did.

We could argue that a couple of mites wouldn't buy anything and so she wasn't out anything. When you're broke you can afford to be generous, or even reckless. But that is begging the point.

Jesus has made it painfully clear: it's all or nothing. That is the only way salvation can be ours. When this price has been paid, a passport into the Kingdom of God is issued, the drawbridge is lowered, the gates are thrown wide open, and the King himself is there to give the greeting: "Welcome home! The Kingdom is yours."

Now, let's switch metaphors and examine these sister parables, so different but so alike.

Good News Is Expensive

THE HIDDEN TREASURE (Matthew 13:44)

During my childhood days, some neighborhood bullies tried to confiscate the ball with which I was playing. Rather than surrender it, I ran away. Sensing that I might not outrun them, I flipped the ball into the woods, carefully noting where it went. Later I returned to the site, searched, and found the ball. That time I actually outwitted them (which wasn't always the case).

Long ago, it was common practice to hide valuables when trouble threatened or erupted. As we know so well, this is what happened to the ancient Essenes as they read the Roman handwriting on their Qumran walls. Regrettably, the tiny community evidently was entirely wiped out with no survivors to tell the world what they had hidden—or where. Quite by accident were these priceless scrolls found nearly two thousand years later.

As Jesus told this parable, his listeners were well acquainted with the laws and customs of the day.

A certain hired man was plowing or cultivating a field —perhaps for the nth time. Suddenly his instrument tore into something buried in the soil. Stopping to examine it, he discovered the dream of a lifetime: a hidden treasure. Carefully covering the treasure with dirt, he nonchalantly continued his work, whistling a merry tune.

Without blabbing to anyone about his incredible find, he quietly went about the task of selling all of his goods. Everything. He was not taking any chances. By law, he could claim the treasure since the statutes said that finders were keepers. Had the owner of the land hidden the treasure himself, he certainly wouldn't have run the risk of his hired man finding it. Therefore, the implication is clear: the treasure had been hidden, probably for quite some time. Even so, the man wasn't taking any chances.

When he had enough, he carefully made an offer—a generous one but not suspiciously reckless—and bought the field. The field, with its invaluable treasure, was his.

No one could question his ethics or rights. No one could blackmail him or conjure up a phony claim. He could even invite witnesses to watch him unveil his treasure, and he could secure it by having an armed guard (probably a plainclothesman) standing by. Whatever, he took no chances. He was not going to lose the opportunity of a lifetime.

Jesus did not tell us who the man is, nor what the treasure represents. Some say that the treasure is Christ, and the man represents anyone who diligently seeks until he finds. This might pass except in all likelihood the hired man was simply doing his job—laborious and hardly very rewarding. He was not looking for a treasure, nor was he expecting to find one. The discovery was quite by accident.

To think that Jesus was saying that if we keep on plodding along we'll find the Great Treasure is to miss the point. This is dubious theology. Admission to the Kingdom is not by luck or happenstance.

Nor was Jesus trying to say that the poor (hired men traditionally have not been rich men) someday will find their reward. Nor is Jesus suggesting that the rich will not get richer (the finder of the pearl, as we shall see, was probably well-off to begin with).

Jesus, however, seems to be making a telling point: if and when you do find the treasure, what will you do about it? Leave it buried in the field? Squander it as the prodigal did? Hang on to it as the rich young ruler chose to do? Throw a big party as the king did for his son?

Even though there are many possibilities, the whole thrust aims at one point: the hired man in no way was going to lose the treasure. Whatever it would take to claim it, he was willing and anxious to do. And he did. He did not procrastinate. He did not bury it to search for a bigger and better discovery. He did not ask the owner of the field for approval. He presumably did not even seek the advice of friends and family. He acted on his own. That is how one becomes a citizen of the Kingdom.

THE COSTLY PEARL (Matthew 13:45, 46)
If the parable of the hidden treasure is a blue-collar parable, this one speaks to the white-collar crowd.

Separately they speak with far less force than when
harnessed together.

A certain entrepreneur made his living importing and
exporting pearls. One day while researching the market,
his attention was drawn toward a rumored pearl of
unusual significance. Acting upon a combination of good
business sense and an educated hunch, he set forth to see
for himself. What he discovered was a sleeper: a pearl
which his skillful eye told him was far more valuable than
anyone realized.

Again, as in the case of the hired man, he acted with
diligence and wisdom, being careful not to tip his hand.
When he had sold everything he owned, he had enough to
bid on the pearl. His bid—either the offered price or an
acceptable down payment—was honored, and the
priceless pearl was his.

What we do not know is not terribly important, but it
is worthy of exploration. He might have had real
difficulty disposing of his property quickly for an
equitable price. He may have had to make some sacrifices.

The competition also might have been formidable. His
bids may have been pushed nearly beyond his reach. This
could have caused him to borrow, but he knew it would
be worth it.

He, too, might have had second thoughts. Was it worth
the risk of selling everything—his home, business, his
lesser favorite pearls? Would his wife think he had gone
berserk, or did he have to quietly dispose of his goods
without her knowledge, knowing he could not get her
consent?

These sentiments have found their way into innumerable cliches: opportunity only strikes once; a chance of a
lifetime; a bird in the hand is worth two in the bush.
And even a famed musical strikes the same theme: once
you have found her, never let her go.

Why did he do it?

There is only one reason. This particular pearl, if
possessed, would be worth far more than what it would
cost. If, for instance, the merchant had sold his entire
estate for $100,000, he knew that he was not purchasing

a pearl worth only a mere $100,000. It would be worth perhaps $500,000 or even more. That is why he had to have it.

Many merchants would not think it wise or profitable to sell off heirlooms and keepsake memories, stocks and bonds, and other possessions merely to gain 10 or 20 percent. But to double or quadruple their investment? Then it might be worth it.

It has been said that Cleopatra, who lived not far removed from this story either in time or space, possessed a pearl worth several millions of dollars.

This enterprising merchant knew his pearls, but he also knew his values. For him, selling everything to get this pearl was everything. He could not sleep until he owned it. If he lost it, he would never forgive himself.

Some seem to feel that these parables were teaching the costliness—the value—of the privilege of being citizens in the Kingdom of God. That is true, in part.

Others feel that these parables taught the high cost of holy living. Although holy living is costly, and self-sacrifice consequential, this is not the essential thought Jesus seems to have had in mind.

What Jesus was saying was that the Kingdom of which he spoke becomes available to people in different ways. Furthermore, it is available to the poorest of blue-collar people as well as the wealthiest white-collar entrepreneurs. Besides, the entrance fee is the same for all: everything. It is within the grasp of anyone and everyone. With no exceptions!

If one is willing to sell everything, it matters not what one nets: $100 or less, $1,000,000 or more. Whatever the sum, it will be adequate to purchase either the land with the treasure or the pearl of great price.

Some, after plodding along through life, will suddenly hear the great news that salvation can be theirs. What rejoicing there is when one surrenders everything to Christ, exchanging grubby work clothes for a garment of righteousness.

Others, after searching an entire life, suddenly discover

that Christ is the answer, that he holds the key, that
eternal life can be a glorious reality. No two come to
Christ in the same way, but all may come.

There are those who feel that these parables are talking
about self-sacrifice, about giving up everything for
Christ. And they are—in a sense.

However, these parables put aside any thought that the
Christian faith is one of empty victory. Many—yes, far too
many—believers either teach or are taught that Christianity
means giving up everything and getting little or nothing
in return (except a vague intangible promise of life
everlasting later, but nothing but a wearisome struggle
now).

This concept was dispelled vigorously by these
parables.

When the hired man finally possessed the treasure, he
was infinitely richer than before. The little he gave up to
obtain the treasure was nothing in comparison.

The same is true of the merchant who in possessing the
pearl of great distinction was richer than before. The pearl
he now owned was worth every penny it cost him,
heirlooms and all.

Jesus wanted us to know that there is no entrance into
the great Kingdom in any other way, and that "whosoever
will" may enter. But he also wanted us to know that the
Christian life is exciting, rewarding, and far better than
the old life. In no way was Jesus saying or implying that
we are to give up a thousand-dollar life for one only
worth twenty-five. Nor was Jesus saying that we are to
give up a thousand-dollar life for one worth eleven
hundred or even two thousand. Rather, we surrender our
rags for his riches. The comparison is not minimal, it's
incredible.

In both of the parables just examined, one more thought
rises to the surface: what did the hired man do with his
treasure, what did the pearl importer do with his pearl?

Did the hired man swap his blue collar for a white one?
If so, was that all he did? Did the businessman retire and
settle for a blue-collared sport shirt?

Did they use their acquisitions to improve their living or help those around them? Did they make wise investments, both of time and money? Did the hired man buy up all the farms in the area to look for more and better treasures? Did the pearl entrepreneur keep searching for an even more priceless pearl?

These are sobering, even haunting questions. Once we have discovered our treasure, what we do with it is of prime importance. What it does to us, also, is extremely important.

Put another way, once we have received Christ as Lord and Savior and have gained entrance into Christendom, the Kingdom of God, what next? Do we simply walk across the drawbridge, show our passport, greet the King, and then find the nearest bench? Or do we begin to explore all the nooks and crannies of the castle, and take advantage of all the marvelous opportunities awaiting at every turn?

Do we walk back over the drawbridge, so to speak, and help others find their treasures and pearls of distinction?

It is one thing to become a believer; it is quite another to move on in the Christian life.

Although Jesus did not say so, it is quite unlikely that the hired man sat at home simply admiring his treasure. It was his, and he could do as he pleased. But unless he did something of consequence with it, he would be of all men most miserable.

The importer, likewise, could have built a strongbox in which to keep his treasured pearl, and even make daily pilgrimages to gaze upon it. Or he could have had it mounted in a museum for everyone to admire. Even then, he probably wouldn't be satisfied unless it was put to work, invested in such a way that it brought credit both to him and his profession.

SECTION TWO

PEOPLE PARABLES

A WORD ABOUT PEOPLE PARABLES

The first twelve chapters of this book are primarily concerned with theological matters. This latter section deals with more practical aspects of everyday living, the main focus of Jesus' "people parables."

These people parables give uncanny insights into human nature. If explored fully, the development of an exciting, authentic manner of living can gradually unfold into a marvelous Christian life-style.

Christians, often grasping for something solid on which to build their personal lives, may be eternally grateful for the unexpected assistance given by these amazing parables.

Deliberately, although not out of necessity, this section is limited to the parables in the Gospel according to Saint Luke, following the same chronological pattern excepting those parables which have already been discussed.

Although this is not an attempt to improve upon the editing procedures of the synoptic writers, the same rights and privileges remain: to use these ingenious stories of the great master storyteller to enrich both our Christian theology and life-style.

CHAPTER THIRTEEN
GRATITUDE—
THE TWO DEBTORS
Luke 7:36-50

Mealtime can be a marvelous experience or a disaster. Jesus experienced both and so have we.

Mealtime can easily be sabotaged by the unexpected. Untimely interruptions have ruined many steaks and even more dispositions. Unforeseen guests have happened by to enrich the blessedness of a stretched table fare, but freeloaders always manage to destroy the sacredness of dinnertime.

Gratitude is one of the most difficult of all graces. It is not always easy to be grateful when feeding ten guests on five pork chops. Even though the refrigerator usually manages to yield a few eggs and yesterday's ham to supplement the too few chops, we still find it difficult to experience genuine gratitude for the privilege of sharing.

On the other hand, it is equally difficult to express gratitude when someone extends a common (or uncommon) courtesy. True gratitude does not always come easily, or readily.

Jesus was Simon's guest, but Jesus probably found it difficult to be genuinely grateful under the unpleasant circumstances.

If one studies the several known dinner experiences of Jesus, it becomes obvious that his mealtime was often exploited. Jesus knew more than once what it was like to be the unwanted guest.

Simon (not Peter), an active Pharisee, had formally invited Jesus to dinner. This was no mere luncheon, but a dinner of the type accorded visiting dignitaries, religious or civil. Because Simon was uncertain regarding the credentials of Jesus, the stranger from Galilee, he was taking no chances. He dared not neglect official protocol extended to visiting rabbis (in case Jesus were an authentic rabbi); and he felt obligated to expose, if necessary and possible, the mystique surrounding the increasingly popular teacher.

But for some reason, Simon neglected to extend Jesus the normal courtesies of hospitality. He did not wash the feet of Jesus, nor did he greet him with the customary kiss, nor did he anoint his head with oil. Jesus, actually the guest of honor, was treated worse than an intruder. He was unwelcome and he knew it.

Since a gathering of this kind was a rather formal affair, it appears likely that as they dined they did not sit on chairs at a table, but reclined on low benches. Strange as it seems to us, it was proper to prop one's head with one hand and eat with the other.

When these receptions for visiting dignitaries were held, it was not uncommon for town folk to enter the house to observe what was happening. However, it was highly irregular for people of questionable repute to enter; but that is exactly what happened.

A townswoman, probably a woman of ill repute, brazenly entered the dining room. She had heard that Jesus was going to be there, and she had to see him once

again to express her appreciation for what he had done
for her previously.

When she saw him reclining at the table, she was
overwhelmed with gratitude. Her overflowing heart
turned into a flood of tears which streamed down her
cheeks, landing on the feet of Jesus. This kind of emotion
cannot be manufactured. No more could this woman turn
on the tears than turn them off.

Then she did something else quite irregular. Not
knowing just what to do as her tears turned the unwashed
feet of Jesus into a mud-streaked spectacle, she unbound
her long hair and with it dried the feet of the one who
had forgiven her sins. Tenderly she smothered the feet of
Jesus with kisses, and then anointed them with an
expensive balm which she had brought with her, hoping
she could present it to him. What gratitude!

By now everyone in the room was watching, especially
Simon, the host. Jesus alone knew exactly what was
happening. When the drama was over, that painfully
awkward moment arrived. When one is overcome with
emotion and acts out of character, it can be terribly
embarrassing and unsettling later. Gratitude is no
exception. This grateful woman, who had made a
spectacle of herself, had also shamed herself by letting
her hair down in public. That just wasn't proper in those
days. Then Jesus took command.

Knowing what Simon, the rascal, was thinking, and
how the poor woman must be feeling, Jesus diverted the
attention away from her toward himself. As she slowly
rose to her feet, her anxieties were short-lived. Jesus,
with gratitude for what she had done—especially in
contrast to what Simon had left undone—broke the
tension by telling another of his timely stories.

There were two debtors who could not pay their
obligations. One owed a relatively small amount, but the
other was ten times as deeply in debt. Both of them,
however, were forgiven and went home debt-free. Then,
turning to Simon, Jesus asked him which of the two was
most grateful.

Simon had no options, and he knew it. He could not

avoid the question nor its implications. Lamely he said
that he supposed it would be the one who was forgiven
the most. Jesus agreed. There the parable ended, but
gratitude never ends. No doubt, during the buzz which
followed this short but dramatic exchange between host
and guest, Jesus quietly walked with the forgiven woman
to the door where she inconspicuously slipped away.

Gratitude is often a lonely virtue. At times it is more
difficult to receive graciously than to give. Occasionally
gratitude gushes forth in a torrent of words or tears.
Sometimes it stays bottled up inside, seeking for a means
of expression adequate to the occasion. If it remains pent
up, like any other emotion it can die; or it can erupt in
some unpredictable way.

Gratitude can express itself in some bizarre behavior,
and it has been known to act anonymously. Consequently,
beneficial ways of releasing gratitude must be found,
either in word or deed or both.

Certain scholars remind us that in the Aramaic, Hebrew,
and Syriac languages there is no precise word for
thankfulness. Therefore, another word is needed, or a
dramatic gesture.

The story is told of a British subject who rescued two
Arabs who had crashed in the desert. To show their
appreciation, the English gentleman, already married,
was offered the greatest gift the two men could give,
their eldest daughters. It was a touching but impossible
gesture, and when graciously declined almost created
an international scene.

There are times when a deed ought to supplement
words. "Say it with flowers" is more than a catchy slogan.
There are, fortunately, countless ways to express
gratitude, including pouring costly cologne on neglected
feet. Unorthodox, perhaps, but highly personal.

Gratitude can also lead into unpleasant or unusual
situations. Simon was building his case against Jesus by
musing that if Jesus were truly a prophet, he would
certainly know the reputation of this woman. But that was

not a very convincing argument. A gentleman would
hardly need to be a prophet to know what she was.

Therefore, as Jesus told this parable about forgiveness,
he was not only destroying Simon's smug argument in the
process; he was defending the newly created status of the
forgiven woman. (Note: the original text implies strongly,
grammatically, that she was forgiven prior to this
encounter in Simon's dining room although many
translations do not make this clear.)

Jesus also knew that creditors usually don't go around
tearing up IOUs. That's why he made this point—not to
teach a rather dubious doctrine of indiscriminate forgiveness (that a Christian always must overlook everything),
but to dramatize that gratitude ought to follow forgiveness. From the parable we do not know if the debtors
were grateful or not. We do know, however, that gratitude
is not automatic. Of the ten lepers cleansed, only one
returned to express thanks.

Jesus also told the parable to remind us that there will
be differing degrees of gratitude, and that there are
various ways of expressing gratefulness. The woman
came prepared with expensive balm with which to anoint
Jesus. She had heard that Jesus would be a guest;
therefore, her act was premeditated (except for the tears
and muddied feet). She dared enter the house, although
she knew it was forbidden to her kind, because her
mission was worth the risk. Her act of gratitude was
carefully planned, as it ought to be, and it was
commensurate with what Christ had done for her.

Since the expression of our gratitude is not always
spontaneous or easy, there are times when we must work
at it. And work overtime.

But what about ingratitude? How is this handled?

Jesus, as previously suggested, probably accepted
hospitality graciously but not gratefully, necessarily.
Too often it has been suggested that a Christian life-style
should always be heavy on meekness. This is subject to
challenge, depending upon the circumstances.

Simon knew better, yet acted childish spiritually. He undoubtedly was among the religious elite in town and probably was a knowledgeable businessman. His home was adequate for entertaining dignitaries, and he certainly knew all the civil and religious common courtesies of Eastern hospitality and protocol. In spite of this, he treated Jesus shamefully; yet seemingly Jesus acted as though nothing were remiss. At times a silent "gratitude" may be in order.

However, Jesus, who also knew the customs of the culture, waited for the opportune moment. When it arrived, he exposed the sham of the hour in a decisive way. To strike when the iron is hot may not always be wise; so Jesus waited. However, he did not wait when he drove the money changers from the Temple, nor did he wait for privacy when rebuking Peter.

When the opportune moment arrived, Jesus seized it, embarrassing his host publicly in his own home for deliberately failing to extend the expected common courtesies.

Ingratitude is a demeaning characteristic, unbecoming to a Christian life-style. Simply defined it means "ungratefulness," but it goes much deeper than that. It is "ungratefulness without feeling or appreciation in a spirit of disagreeableness." To be forgiven and live with ingratitude is a miserable way to live.

On the other hand, to merely tolerate ingratitude or simply shrug it off is also a wretched way to live. Wisely, but firmly—in the manner of Jesus—we should rebuke ingratitude. A word to the wise may be sufficient, but others may need more than a gentle whisper.

The woman who risked her already tarnished name to express her personal appreciation in a tangible way had to do so. She couldn't have lived with herself with all those tears of gratitude welling up within her. She had to return to her Savior—in a culture where deeds were more important than words—to once again express her deepest gratitude. She was in the early stages of building a beautiful Christian life-style.

CHAPTER FOURTEEN
HOSPITALITY—
THE PERSISTENT
MIDNIGHT NEIGHBOR
Luke 11:5-8

While living in Europe we noticed that people often shopped daily, purchasing only enough for a meal or two. Refrigerators were smaller, and often "undernourished."

When a couple of American students stayed with one of our parishioners for a few days, they became hungry one late evening and decided to raid the icebox. To their surprise, it was virtually bare. Evidently their host ate when the need arose, but only with what he could get easily from the corner grocery. Reluctantly, these students gently closed the door on their hunger (the cupboard also was bare), fell asleep, and awakened to a well-prepared breakfast seemingly plucked out of the sky.

Moving further eastward and back a couple thousand years, it would not be unusual for the cupboard to be bare at midnight. Bread was baked each day before sunrise and was often gone by evening.

Because of several children and dark evenings, the neighbor Jesus was talking about had by midnight been in bed for several hours. That is when he heard the gentle rapping which soon turned into pounding. Sufficiently irritated by now, the sleepy householder whispered a brusque, "Go away!" Finally, after some persuasion, the persistent neighbor was given some hard rolls and sent on his way.

The interesting thing in this parable is that Jesus did not suggest that this happened. Rather, Jesus asked his listeners if they could ever imagine such a reluctant response. The answer, of course, was negative.

Hospitality at that time in that part of the world was as much a part of their culture as breathing. To be inhospitable, especially after a long, hard journey, was inconceivable. Hospitality was sacred.

Jesus made his point. Since he was actually talking about prayer at the time, he was saying that it is just as inconceivable to think of God as a reluctant, sleepy neighbor who must be jolted awake and hounded into hearing and answering prayer.

As in many of the parables, there are subdominant although important messages. In this particular story, hospitality is one of them. Christian hospitality too often rises and falls on the whims of its culture, failing to stand on its own understanding. In certain settings, the Christian life-style knows little or nothing about a personal, natural form of hospitality but practices an excellent formal or official hospitality.

This kind of entertaining can be a marvelous, meaningful experience. Welcoming (or farewell) committees often create unforgettable evenings which range from pure elegance to artificial exhibitionism. Unfortunately, these official gatherings often rob individuals and families of a spontaneous or premeditated personal hospitality which in some circles has become almost a lost art.

Christian hospitality, rediscovered in other situations, has resulted in a variety of programs, including

fellowship dinners, tea-drenched happy hours, friendship
evangelism, and neighborhood coffee Bible studies. Some
of this seems to be the result of an emptiness felt
(consciously or otherwise) because of believers wanting
to stop avoiding hospitality coupled with a need to
evangelize more naturally.

In the first century, hospitality was an integral part
of the culture, probably stemming back to Abraham or
even earlier. But alas, the early Christians seemed to run
off in opposite directions. In some cases they became
freeloaders and gluttons, refusing to share with others; in
other cases they became too hospitable to runaways and
dissidents. Some were indifferent to hospitality and were
chided for their neglect.

Hospitality, like gratitude, is hardly automatic, and it
can be risky business. Christians and non-Christians alike
can and do exploit the hospitable. Being hospitable can
result in tremendous inner satisfaction, and it can bring
considerable pain. Hospitality, for many, is a sheer
struggle or just plain drudgery, but it also can get into the
blood.

Now back to the parable for some observations on
hospitality. Jesus, first of all, is asking if we can imagine
anyone, especially a neighboring friend, who would turn
us down in an hour of need. Regrettably, today, the
answer is yes! Hospitality is something that never can be
taken for granted. Even though hospitality was practiced
to such a degree that no one could imagine a person
refusing to entertain a stranger much less a friend, it did
not take very long in the early church before hospitality
began to die out.

Hospitality rises and falls from culture to culture. Some
peoples are much more given to it than others, traditionally or out of necessity. Hospitality, as a part of a
Christian life-style, also rises and falls with its culture.
One wonders if this is the way it ought to be. On the other
hand, in some circles, a casual invitation or a hospitable
gesture can be badly mistaken. Even so, the implication is
exceptionally strong that Jesus would prefer a Christian

life-style which is surprised when hospitality is not
extended rather than when it is.

We also see another incongruity which we could call a
crisis hospitality. Christians respond marvelously (and
so do others) during a crisis. In this parable there was a
crisis. A traveler arrived, hungry, dusty, and weary after a
hard journey. He knew that he would be welcome and
given a comfortable bed after a midnight snack. He could
expect, and would expect, three hard rolls and a little
wine with which to wash it down. The host, however, had
no bread and was obligated to find some. Thinking that
his neighbor might have a little left over, he quickly ran
next door.

Often it takes but a little to be hospitable—a quick run
to the neighbor's, a cup of coffee and a sweet roll.
Hospitality need not involve the killing of the fatted calf,
although at times this is expected and in order. A crisis
hospitality, fortunately, can lead to bigger and better
things, and often does.

It has often been said that hospitality begins at home. It
does. It is quite inconceivable to think of the traveler
coming to the home of a friend who shrugs his shoulder,
saying, "Sorry, friend. I don't have a thing in the house
to eat. But if you will go over to my neighbor, I'm sure he
can help you out." Hospitality can quickly degenerate
into a passing the buck type of situation, and it does. But
in the biblical situation, the host, embarrassed and
distressed because he desperately wants to help, wouldn't
think of passing the buck. He went himself and hounded
his neighbor until he produced what he needed. Where
there's a will there's a way, even in the art of hospitality.

Being hospitable does have its risks. The host in this
parable ran the risk of losing a friendship; in fact, two of
them. The traveler was entitled to three rolls and a bit of
wine, but if he were unreasonable, as some people are, he
might have expected—or demanded—a three-course
meal, even at midnight. Some people are difficult if not
impossible to please, and any hospitality given them must
be given grudgingly or at least reluctantly.

Hospitality—The Persistent Midnight Neighbor

What happens when guests are inconsiderate, boorish, ill-mannered, reeking with ingratitude? What would Jesus do if he were entertaining ill-mannered guests? Probably the same thing he did to the rude Pharisee who invited him to dinner without extending any of the common courtesies. Yes, there were and are limitations to the art of hospitality.

No doubt the traveler was deeply grateful for the three rolls, whether or not he knew the predicament he caused. Besides, the one who reluctantly gave up the leftover rolls (the neighboring host could have asked him for some lamb chops and wine) could return to dreamland, but his neighbor had to stay up, engage in conversation, fix a place for his guest to sleep, and bed down his guest's donkey. Then, and only then, could he return to his interrupted sleep (he, too, was probably awakened unexpectedly).

If there are limitations on hospitality, and there are, what happens when the cupboard is bare? Must one share when there is nothing to share? Although it is impossible, and unwise, to build a case on this from the parable at hand, there is something important said indirectly.

The word "importunity" (verse 8) is rarely used, either in Scripture or in our daily vocabularies. Generally, the word means "stubbornness or unreasonable persistence." If so, the host might have badly irritated his sleeping neighbor.

However, there is another dimension to the word as used in this setting: shamelessness. This makes a significant difference. When the word "importunity" is linked to hospitality, it is not as much a stubborn or unreasonable persistence as it is a sense of shame if one is not hospitable. Therefore, the host should not be embarrassed if forced to remedy a situation at midnight, but he should feel a sense of shame if he didn't. Importunity literally forced him to do what was necessary to be hospitable, even to the point of borrowing.

We find it difficult in the West to understand Eastern hospitality precisely at this point of shamelessness. When

the art of being hospitable is a sacred trust, one should
and does feel ashamed when violating it. We could argue
that this was not necessarily a Christian virtue, so why
stress it? This would be rational except that even though
Jesus was not directly teaching hospitality in the parable,
it wasn't long after this that the early Christians were
severely chided for their lack of hospitality.

As a finale, let me suggest what could be called a
rational hospitality. This might be more clearly seen in its
antithesis: an irrational hospitality. Entertaining simply
because it is a Christian duty could be counterproductive.
People, with a built-in radar system for detecting genuine
and selfless behavior, could easily end up with a good
dinner but no real hospitality.

Geographical hospitality is also troublesome. In certain
cultures, no one ever enters another person's home except
by invitation. Then, when this formality has been
accomplished, a second invitation cannot be extended
until the first is reciprocated. To apply a totally different
cultural pattern, ignoring the local situation, could create
more problems than imaginable. Sound reasoning, a
gentle sensitivity, and appreciation of cultural and
regional traits will produce hospitality, but it must be a
rational hospitality.

Early in my ministry, I quickly discovered within my
own small parish that as pastor I was welcome in certain
homes at any time, but in others I was only welcome if I
had previously made an appointment. Why? Various
regional and cultural levels of sophistication (and
pseudosophistication) dictate. I learned to live with it and
found no insurmountable barriers to a rational hospitality.

Economic hospitality is also a challenge. In the parable,
we are not told why the host had no bread. Since no
preservatives were used, most of the bread was eaten
during the same day in which it was baked. This may
have been the case. He may also have been a very poor
man. Somehow he was able to choose a neighbor who did
have some leftover food. There are times when entertaining poses a serious problem.

Hospitality—The Persistent Midnight Neighbor

Early in our ministry in Sweden, we decided to entertain as freely as possible in our home but with a couple of reservations. The first was that we would keep it simple (coffee parties, simple meals). We also decided not to purchase expensive bakery items. Rather, Barbara would bake and freeze, within reason, so that we would be ready for the unexpected as well as the planned. Then we agreed that we would entertain unorthodoxly; that is, neither typical Swedish or American, but perhaps a combination of the two or in some other style (we were engaged in a multinational ministry with people from over sixty different countries). Finally, we agreed that we would use this simple style hospitality as a part of our ministry and continue it until we ran out of money. We never ran out although we averaged about two guests per day during our three-year tenure.

In the parable of the good Samaritan, the hospitality was not administered in a home but in an inn. This, no doubt, was out of practical necessity. Again, although this does not prove any point, it does suggest another option. For various reasons, some are able, and prefer, to entertain outside the home. Homes can be too small, or too far away, but they can never be too humble.

Mary and Martha also say something about hospitality protocol. Martha, so intent on serving Jesus a good meal, found out that she was not serving him well. It was not her concern for the hunger of Jesus that earned the rebuke; it was her preoccupation with the kitchen. Mary was commended, not because she left all the culinary concerns to Martha, but because she emphasized a more noble form of hospitality.

Hospitality essentials can and often do obscure the purpose of entertaining. Being chained to a stove, fretting over the inadequacies of a stubborn roast can dampen the best of premeditated motives. Mary was able to break with the standard protocol as she neglected her usual kitchen responsibilities to spend time with the honored guest. Modifications can and ought to be made when practicing hospitality. Perhaps a spot of tea or donuts and coffee would be more suitable with certain guests, particularly if the purpose of entertaining is not to impress but to be hospitable. Whatever, Jesus endorsed what Mary was doing, and she was violating the letter of the law, perhaps, but more importantly, kept the spirit.

The rules and regulations of proper hospitality protocol and entertaining etiquette are complicated, not only now, but they always have been. Jesus, in many ways, was rather unorthodox in this matter. He ate with publicans and sinners. He accepted invitations to dinner traps and endured numerous social fiascoes. He refused to scold Mary for neglecting Martha in her hour of need, and served his disciples breakfast on the shores of the Sea of Galilee. He ate and ran (in Emmaus). He used the "last supper" to announce his betrayer. He instituted the breaking of bread and drinking of wine as a perpetual memorial, and early in the life of the church, potlucks and love feasts were not uncommon.

Jesus seems not to burden us with a rigidity in making hospitality a part of our Christian life-style. Whether it's a room at the Hilton or a rollaway in the den—whether it's a sumptuous banquet or some hard rolls with a jar of jam—it matters not. What Jesus does want is that we give a cup of cold water in his name.

Remember, Jesus isn't surprised when Christians are hospitable. He is surprised—and grieved—when Christians are inhospitable.

CHAPTER FIFTEEN
BRINKMANSHIP—
SETTLING OUT
OF COURT
Luke 12:54-59

Years ago, when I was barely a teenager, we had some dead time to fill between the afternoon youth meeting and the evening service. Since the church was located near a rather large river, one of our pastimes included walking across the bridge, high above the river—not on the sidewalk but on the balustrade.

Per usual, not very far away lurked a daredevil. His specialty was not merely walking the foot-wide span; his defiance was to walk as near the outer edge as possible. We, who were younger, were expected to follow or run the risk of being branded chicken.

Either I was scared or had better judgment, I'm not sure, but I refused to play the game.

Brinkmanship—the dubious art of living dangerously— is suggested by this parable. Within every person there are varying degrees of recklessness, timidity, common sense, and fear. Some carefully plan ahead, but others operate by impulse or out of necessity. While many head down the center of the road of life, others meander about as an undisciplined, inquisitive dog on a stroll with its master.

Jesus was talking to a crowd when for some reason he exploded in what seems to be a burst of irritation. In using the uncomplimentary "You hypocrites!" he certainly wasn't trying to impress them or create goodwill. He was verbally knocking their heads together.

Why? Because his audience was intelligent enough to check the skies to predict the weather—red sky at night, sailor's delight—but not discerning enough to see where it was heading. The nation was unmistakably heading for disaster, but was blind to the symptoms; the same was true individually. What angered Jesus, and gave him so much sorrow, was the fact that they chose to be blind. Not only were these people walking the balustrade, they were doing a jig on it, blindfolded.

Having now secured their attention (call someone a hypocrite and a response is virtually guaranteed), Jesus drove home another parable. In short, Jesus told the guilty crowd that he wanted to give them some advice. "Rather than letting your adversary take you to court, why don't you try to settle out of court?" Once the judge's gavel fell, there was no turning back. When the trial was over, the judge would make a decision and the one found guilty would be turned over to the officer for imprisonment or punishment.

Jesus, as we examine his concern, seems to be referring both to the personal and national judgment of the people. The Romans were already breathing heavily down their necks, and within a short time the Jews' nation actually ceased to exist, crushed by a fanatic and ruthless power. No wonder Jesus desperately wanted to get their attention in order to divert them from their brinkmanship. The ones he came to warn were the ones who refused to listen. Jesus knew they would pay, and pay dearly (every last penny)

if they didn't change their ways, but they had flirted with
disaster for too long.

Brinkmanship is a dangerous game people play, and as
a Christian life-style it leaves much to be desired. Russian
roulette is hardly new, but it is no less dangerous than
when first invented.

Brinkmanship can be caused by putting off important
affairs until it's too late, flirting with destiny. The ancient
Jews, whom Jesus desperately tried to warn, gambled on
their destiny and lost.

We now seem to be living in an era of suit-craziness.
At the drop of a hat, someone can get hauled into court.
Friends agree to a lawsuit and divide the spoils later.
Brothers and sisters contest a will and remain enemies
forever. Doctors refuse to give emergency aid for fear of a
malpractice suit, and costs skyrocket because of phony
claims.

Consequently, many of us know what Jesus was talking
about when he advocated settling out of court. Once a trial
begins, the judge's decision is final. Today we live with
appeals and courts of appeal. This can muddy the concept
Jesus was stressing, but in the imagery of the parable,
there was no appeal possible. This is why Jesus advocated
settling in advance.

As usual, the parable gives only the barest of details.
Consequently, it is necessary to reconstruct a typical,
probable, and believable scene. Suppose that a creditor
had in good faith loaned money to a young businessman
for the purpose of establishing an import-export business.
During his travels abroad searching for potential
imports, the young man squandered the borrowed money,
refusing later to repay the negotiated loan. Several
options were open, legally. However, the creditor, a
reasonable man, sought every way possible to collect his
money, but was thwarted by the wily young debtor who
used every dodge he could think of.

The creditor's final recourse was to sue him in court.
Discovering that the young debtor was guilty, the judge

would sentence him accordingly. The youthful offender would then go to prison until every penny was repaid. If family and friends wouldn't or couldn't pay his debts, he would rot in jail.

However, as the debtor was being escorted to court, he came to his senses. Now he had several options. He could do as the young prodigal did: rehearse a plea of forgiveness and hope that mercy would follow. He could attempt to escape and become a fugitive the rest of his life. Or he could try to get his family and friends to pay the debt.

The most sensible thing to do would be to stop the proceedings of the court before the trial began. This would mean that the young man would have to get into immediate contact with his accuser, persuade him to listen to his plea, come up with an offer, and sell the creditor on his newfound reasonableness and penitence.

No matter which pathway he chose, he had to settle it on the way to the judge's chambers or it would be too late. Even the creditor couldn't forgive or extend credit then.

As it turned out, the young entrepreneur was able to convince the creditor of his sincerity. So the creditor listened to the alternative proposal and gave the young man a second chance. All of this was done while standing in the heat of the day outside the judge's chamber. That is brinkmanship!

Does this idea of brinkmanship preclude any idea of living dangerously? Does it mean that the ideal Christian life-style ought to avoid or shun that which is hazardous or risky? Should all Christians be squeezed into a conservative life-style? Hardly. Not if the term conservative means merely moderation, prudence, cautiousness.

The young debtor was forced into taking a risk in order to avoid a greater risk. Risk-taking, or brinkmanship, simply as a style of life, could be ridiculous. But it does not mean that there are never any occasions when a Christian won't be forced to the brink. It is at this point that the parable seems clear. Jesus suggested that the

matter should be settled *on the way* to court. Although it
is better late than never, it would be erroneous to say that
Jesus was advocating brinkmanship. He wasn't, but he
was encouraging the use of every possible moment, even
the last, just as he was discouraging the absurdity of
giving up easily or prematurely.

The Christian life-style, then, should not be based on
brinkmanship, but it should be realistic enough to match
wits with any situation. Just as the young debtor as shown
matched wits with his creditor, so should the Christian
use every ounce of ingenuity to stand up to any adversary.
For some, this means that there will be crises demanding
every available source of energy and ingenuity. For
others, whose lives are far less furious, for those who live
much more cautiously and plan considerably ahead, a
crisis life-style is unnecessary, and perhaps even
impossible.

If Jesus wanted his audience to heed the signs of the
times as well as what he was advocating, he must have
had a reason for it. The reason is quite clear. As a people,
the Jews were heading for extreme difficulty. Within
fifty years, it would all be over. Jesus knew this, and he
was trying desperately to forestall, not forecast, their
doom.

Jesus also was ushering in the Kingdom of God. He
knew that the task was enormous, the laborers few.
Therefore, he was pleading for his audience not to wait
until the last moment, but to get on with the work at hand.
Jesus knew the absurdity of trying to pay a debt while
in prison. Today, perhaps, a prisoner may be able to earn
a sizable amount as an author or artist, but in those times
his earning power was zero as he languished in prison.

In all fairness, we must state that Jesus was not only
warning against the dread of the future, he was pleading
for manpower—or as some would prefer, peoplepower.
Never has the call to discipleship been merely an
invitation to escape eternal judgment; it has always been
a clarion call to service. As time runs out on an individual
or a nation, it is also running out on prospects for the

Kingdom. Jesus came "to seek and save those who are lost." This includes warning against pending disaster, but that is only a part of it.

If brinkmanship is flirting with disaster, and it is, it is also something else which we will call bravado. Bravado is false bravery, a defiant or swaggering show of courage. This, too, is a negative form of a Christian life-style, but seemingly there are many who play the game.

If, in the extended parable of the young debtor, we could read his motives, we might find out why he so artistically dodged his creditor. It might have been a cover-up for his failure to establish a successful import-export business. He had a good time wasting the capital, but not such a good time living it down. He had all the earmarks of success, but nothing to show for it. His brinkmanship might have been nothing but a bit of dangerous bravado.

There is also another dimension to brinkmanship which might be called the best of two worlds. This poor young debtor wanted to have his cake and eat it too. He wanted to be a successful entrepreneur and a playboy at the same time. He wanted to impress his foreign friends as well as those back home. He wanted to travel now, pay later.

Why did so many in the audience of Jesus reject his teachings? Why did so few drop everything in order to follow him? One major reason is that they wanted to be the possessors of the best of two worlds, but Jesus said this was impossible. They didn't want to let the one go in order to take hold of the other. Some tried desperately to live near the edge so they could engage in both, depending upon the circumstances. This kind of brinkmanship is not only risky, it is ridiculous and totally unsatisfying. "How," argued Jesus, "can a person serve two masters?" He can't. He'll always favor one over the other.

If we are to avoid flirting with danger, perhaps a word should be said about the other extreme: overcautiousness. This life-style is quite the opposite of that which

encourages one to eat, drink, and be merry, for tomorrow
we die! Gambling on eternal life in order to sow a few
wild oats is hardly worth the risk. But living such an
isolated, sheltered life that insecurity becomes almost a
mania is also a problem.

We see this also in the extended parable of the young
debtor. Suppose he had desired to borrow money for an
import-export business, but then was afraid to run the risk
of searching for salable items or panicked at the prospect
of traveling abroad. To preserve his investment, he placed
it securely in a safe-deposit box. He might be able to repay
his creditor, sans interest perhaps (and living expenses
at home), but an importer-exporter he would not become.

Some Christians are called to a life-style of austerity as
monks or ascetics. Others, for reasons of insecurity
(quite the opposite of brinkmanship), become religious
workaholics. They come early and leave late. They
seldom miss a service and literally work out their own
salvation with fear and trembling. Many of these persons
mean well, but often become prey to various sorts of
religious diversions. The cults and "isms" are full of
people who, insecure and/or unfulfilled by their meagre
life-style, find solace elsewhere.

Development of an authentic Christian life-style is not
always possible at the last minute. Perhaps it never can
be possible although a person can be saved "as by fire."
Foxhole conversions do exist, as well as deathbed
triumphs over eternal death. But these are not the primary
concerns of this parable. Jesus, irritated, frustrated, and
perhaps even angry, couldn't bear the thought of seeing
his own people trampled by the godless Roman army.
Even his persuasiveness couldn't save the day. More than
this, Jesus was grieved because those he had called to
expand the Kingdom of God wanted no part in it. The real
heart of the matter, however, seems to be revealed in two
words: "You hypocrites!"

As concerned as Jesus was for the destiny of his own
people, as compelled as he was to recruit workers to help
do the work he was called to do, that which grieved him

most was their hypocrisy. They pretended to be something they were not.

This life-style—hypocrisy—could well be the most dangerous form of brinkmanship there is. Pretense can lead one to the point of no return more assuredly than either procrastination or bravado.

Pretense is a deceiver. After practicing deception for awhile, or living in a state of not realizing that one is actually a pretender, the difference between faith and fantasy becomes blurred. Many well-meaning people live extremely decent, even good, lives. But there is something missing: there is no positive commitment to Jesus Christ as Lord and Savior of their lives. A whole lifetime can pass, including hundreds of worship services attended, Scriptures read and even memorized, church membership, and even the teaching of little ones, without a commitment.

Those in the crowd Jesus was addressing included the cream of the crop religiously, but Jesus couldn't reach them to point out the futility of their religiosity. Others were simple folk, good people who would never be discourteous or inhospitable, but they too were not followers of Jesus. It is this brinkmanship that is extremely difficult to overcome. In fact, Jesus himself was unsuccessful. If he wept over Jerusalem then, imagine what he did when his entire people were crushed a few years later. Brinkmanship is a game people and nations play, but it is more than that. It becomes a style of life, but a losing life-style.

CHAPTER SIXTEEN
INTERCESSION—
THE BARREN
FIG TREE
Luke 13:1-9

At times there is an exceedingly fine line between interference and intervention, between meddling and mediating. Developing a life-style which is sensitive to this distinction is crucial. There are times when we ought to mind our own business, but there are also times when we must intercede on the behalf of others.

We were riding a London double-decker late one evening when a couple of loudmouths, out of control with alcohol, came aboard. One of them was unbelievably abusive toward an elderly woman, who, incidentally, held her own ground. The bus was overcrowded and the farther we traveled, the more abusive they became. After some blocks, they each lit up in the nonsmoking level. This was all my indignation could tolerate.

Catching the eye of one of them, I suggested that he

extinguish his illegal fire. That did it. He turned his
wrath on me, and I became the target of his abuse with
threats of what would happen when I got off the bus. My
children, teenagers, witnessed this with disbelief, and
with visions of the pounding their dear old dad would
soon be getting.

As I saw their fear, I held my tongue (which wasn't
easy), although at this point I hadn't said much except
for the initial suggestion. Having had quite a bit of
experience with alcohol-induced bravery during my days
in the military, on skid row, in dormitories, and
elsewhere, I recognized his bravado. Even so, I didn't
need a fight, and my poor family needed it less. When our
stop appeared, we quietly exited and the boys never
missed us—nor we them.

To this day I have a scar received in boot camp when I
was forced into a fight because the company bully was
picking on my best friend. I suppose I should have
learned a lesson—that intercession can be a dangerous
thing, that there is a time to intercede and a time not to
intercede. Perhaps I have. But this I do know: the art of
cultivating an intercessory sensitivity is a life-long
struggle.

In the previous chapter we saw among other things the
danger of procrastination and pretense, a gambling
against the future. Now we see more clearly why Jesus was
concerned. If we put off making the paramount decision
and doing the most important thing there is, there will be
no time or energy to get the job done. Productivity is
paramount! A fruit tree which bears no fruit is worthless
and ought to be cut down, since shade is not needed and it
is taking nourishment from the vineyard.

To better understand the setting of this parable, a
journey back into history might be helpful. Job, an upright
man in every way, was accused by the adversary, Satan.
The wily one came up with a shrewd proposal which God
accepted. Satan wanted to prove that the only reason Job
was upright was that he was blessed with a marvelous
family, riches, prestige.

God said that was not true, and so the duel began: Satan
vs. Job. So came the ordeal in which Job was stripped of
his wealth, family, and health. Suffering enormously, Job,
because of his bodily affliction, went outside the city
walls and deposited himself in the local city dump. It was
there his so-called comforting friends came to pay their
respects and condolences. Respectfully, they suffered
with Job in silence for seven days. Then they began their
sermons of comfort, which actually were critical
arguments. Basically his friends argued with Job that the
reason he was suffering was the same reason anyone
suffers: sin. Suffering, pain, anguish, tragedy was God's
way of punishing sins, obvious as well as hidden.

Job wouldn't buy this theology and demanded that they
show him his transgression. They artfully dodged his
rebuttal by insisting that it must be some hidden but
serious sin. Job, knowing his accusers personally and
intimately, knew that they were notorious although
sophisticated sinners themselves; and if suffering were
the direct result of specific sins, these men would be
much worse off than he. Therefore, Job continued to argue
that suffering isn't necessarily the result of a person's
iniquity. If this were true, how could one account for the
material blessings that fall upon the godless?

History repeats itself in odd ways. At the time of this
parable, this same fallacy was believed by the people.
Certain individuals, probably Galileans, were eager to
inform Jesus that some of their fellowmen had been
brutally murdered by Pilate. Even worse, their blood had
been mingled with blood of animals that had been
sacrificed, a horrifying sacrilege.

Jesus, perceiving their self-righteousness, told them
bluntly that these men did not die because they were so
much more wicked than the other Galileans. This old
concept refuses to die and is much alive even today. Jesus
added, in case they didn't get the message, that God
doesn't operate in that fashion and pulled a headline from
the current scene. Evidently word had just informed them
that a certain tower in Siloam had collapsed, killing

eighteen innocent bystanders. Jesus told these Galileans
that the victims' life-style had nothing to do with the
accidental toppling of the tower. It was circumstantial,
not providential.

It was in this context that Jesus released this parable.
This time the hero was the antithesis to these heartless
souls who actually but mistakenly believed that God
punishes unrighteousness and rewards righteousness on
the spot.

This parable is a charmer, especially in contrast to its
setting. A certain landowner evidently loved figs and
decided to plant a select tree in a corner of his vineyard.
Unfortunately no figs grew on the tree, and after several
years the landowner ordered its destruction. His hired
man, however, made a plea for the barren tree, asking
permission to personally try one more time to get some
results. He promised to give the tree special attention;
then, if there were no figs, the owner could destroy it.

There the parable ends. We do not know if the owner
granted the vinedresser's request, but it is assumed that
he did. What we do know is this: the vinedresser was a
man of compassion, a positive thinker who probably
pushed his hope for the barren tree beyond his own
dreams. It was not his tree, but he treated it as though it
were. What a contrast to the smug, self-righteous accusers
who had little or no compassion for fellow Galileans who
were killed in cold blood (perhaps revolutionaries,
executed as a warning to other dissidents).

The vinedresser, a man skilled in raising fruit, must
have known that a tree barren for at least three years must
certainly be permanently fruitless. Why did he care? Why
did he intercede? It wasn't his tree. It wasn't his fault.
It wasn't even his responsibility any more.

Here again we can only speculate. Perhaps he liked a
challenge. Here was a chance for him to test new theories
(digging and fertilizing a fig tree, we are told, was not
customary in those days). He had nothing to lose, not even
his own neck or reputation. Although he limited himself
to a single year, we get the image of two interested men

making regular pilgrimages to see how the pampered tree was doing.

Perhaps he was a man who favored the underdog. Here was a tree which was barren for at least three years (possibly six if the ancient Levitical law was in effect, Leviticus 19:23). It is this spirit of rooting for the underdog that is so important in developing a life-style of compassion and intercession. We discover rather quickly in life that everyone sooner or later begins to hate a perennial winner, or at least dislikes those who win too easily and too often. When, however, we find someone who pulls for the loser and intercedes on behalf of the underdog, our admiration grows.

Perhaps he liked figs, too. If so, his heartbeat was synchronized with that of his employer. It would have been much easier to simply axe the worthless tree, especially if he didn't care for figs—or for his boss. He knew that the tree was absorbing valuable nutrients from the soil, giving nothing in return; but he also knew the exquisite possibilities if he could get the tree to produce. There might have been visions of sweet figs dancing in his head.

Whatever the motives, the vinedresser not only interceded on behalf of the barren tree, he was successful in pleading its case—and his.

A Christian life-style without a concern for the underdog, without feeling for innocent victims (Siloam tower accident) or less than innocent martyrs (the slain Galileans), without a willingness to plead or even fight for the rights and privileges of others, is missing an important ingredient: intercession. When Christians fail to stoop to help the fallen, neglect giving a second chance, forego sharing a cup of cold water or ignore common courtesies and avoid being given to hospitality, it is difficult if not impossible to experience the joys of a bountiful life-style.

We live in a shrinking world with increasingly effective means of reporting news and manipulating masses. It is increasingly difficult to maintain a

reasonable sensitivity when such a desensitizing process
is potential and in progress. Violence, so unnecessary to
many plots and so overly explicit, runs rampant. (My
absence of more than three years from American
television and cinema brought about a chilling plunge
into the visual scene.) Curious and dubious claims of the
so-called "redemptive factor" (e.g., violence is
therapeutic, explicit sex is educational, aberrations are
facts of life) cause one to wonder what Jesus would say in
light of what he said to the desensitized Galileans who
also justified violence but for other reasons.

When jumbo jets collide . . . when crazed dictatorial
powers execute seemingly at will . . . when young teens
are sold into a pitiful and often pitiless prostitution . . .
when law courts are tied in knots because of an inability
to distinguish between liberty and libertinism . . . when
theological prodigals defy reason as well as righteousness,
the maintenance of a spirit of intercession becomes
difficult if not impossible for many.

We get the same feeling another vinedresser may have
had: Why should I care? What can I do about it? It isn't
my fault! Planes will crash, dictators will rule, little girls
will go on selling their bodies, courts will be stymied,
and clergymen will continue abusing their calling. So
what! It's beyond me. Besides, maybe they asked for it.

This is precisely the problem Jesus was attacking. The
people had developed a hardened life-style; they had
lost their sensitivity; they had lost their hope, crushed by
a ruthless oppressor. They felt that if something ill befell
their fellowmen, they must have had it coming; if not,
they were powerless to do anything about it. Eighteen
innocent people crushed into eternity brought no real
anguish, no compassion, no concern that it might happen
elsewhere.

Jesus, who must have felt like throwing up his hands in
horror and disgust, wasted no time in rebuking them for
their insensitivity and lack of compassion. Then, as they
were stunned by his severity, Jesus took the stony silence
and filled it with a tender, compassionate story of a

simple vinedresser who had compassion for a worthless
fig tree. The sobering hush has been felt around the world
as these people reexamined their life-style and we review
ours.

Little did these people realize how insensitive they had
become and how sensitive the interceding vinedresser
was. They couldn't care less; he couldn't care more.

CHAPTER SEVENTEEN
PRETENSE—
THE NARROW DOOR
THAT WAS CLOSED
Luke 13:22-30

Pretense—ranging from a rather harmless world of make-believe to the dangerous profession of premeditated deception—is a game many people play, including believers. In fact, for many it is a life-style.

Living in a world of fantasy may be permissible if it is only a temporary existence, but—as we shall see in the next chapter—we must be pretty realistic most of the time. *Pretense* (a false appearance intended to deceive) is closely akin to *pretend* (to make believe) and *pretext* (an ostensible—outwardly apparent—excuse).

It was this knotty subject Jesus addressed in this complicated passage reported by the physician-turned-writer. Some scholars find no parable at all in this text. Rather than argue, we will agree that it is a difficult passage, a mixture of simile, interrogation, and dialogue held together by current events and eschatology, fused into a unique parabolic story.

Now, having said this, let's reconstruct the scene. Jesus had been traveling from village to village, teaching, preaching, healing, chiding, admonishing, even arguing. He spoke privately with his disciples, publicly to the crowds. He spoke tenderly to the innocent, but spared no invectives with the pretenders.

Now and then Jesus was asked deceptive questions designed to make him look like a buffoon. He was also interrogated with sincere, even naive, questions. On this occasion someone asked a question, but we can only guess its motive based on the answer it received.

The question, "Lord, will only a few be saved?" was not answered directly. The response went something like this: "I wouldn't worry too much about how many will be saved. Just be sure you are, because there will be many who won't be saved."

Instead of answering the question yes or no, Jesus used it as a springboard to say something of vital importance, both to the one who asked the question as well as to those who were listening. Let me, if I may, take the liberty of rephrasing the response:

A certain visitor came among you, inviting you all to his home. You listened, asked questions, and even had a meal or two with him. Then the stranger departed with the invitation still open but ignored.

After awhile, when the time on the invitation had run out, you decided to see what it was all about. As you arrived at the stranger's house, you discovered that the door was closed, bolted from within (evidently because the latch string had been withdrawn, the sign that the door is locked). You pounded on the door and begged the householder to let you in. He refused, saying he did not know who you were.

You then reminded him of the time he visited your village, when he had taught in your streets, when he had even eaten a couple of meals with you. But the stranger within simply could not recall who you were and told you to move on.

As he said this, he reminded you that you had had your

chance. Then he told you to look inside through the
window. When you did, you saw Abraham, Isaac, Jacob,
and the prophets. He also said that if you would look
further you would see all kinds of other people in there,
from east and west, north and south, sitting at the banquet
table.

Then, if you remember, he told you to go ahead and
grind your teeth and weep your hearts out because you
realized that you were on the outside, unable to get in.
Finally he told you that you heard the invitation long
before many of those who were celebrating on the inside,
but you chose to ignore it. Now it's too late.

The tone of this answer—a rather curious parable at that—
indicates that the questioner was one who had failed to
take Jesus seriously, who found reasons not to believe,
who was asking a question merely to feign interest or
impress the crowd. Here is pretense at its peak.

This discourse of Jesus is stern: "You had your chance
—the door was open, but now it's shut forever!" They
didn't bother to respond to the invitation until time had
run out. Then they pretended to be good friends with the
householder, hoping that their buddy-buddy relationship
would unlatch the door—but it didn't.

The question we must ask is this: Why did they wait so
long? What was their excuse?

Other parables have suggested reasonable answers to
why they waited so long before responding to the
invitation. They were too busy; they were preoccupied
with their farms and businesses; they failed to take the
visiting rabbi seriously; they planned poorly; they took
shortcuts; they were uninterested in eternal matters.
Besides, they had their own religion and were not
particularly interested in switching over or even
assimilating new ideas, nor were they interested in any
internal reforms. Even though Jesus drew unprecedented
crowds, silenced his critics, performed miracles, blessed
little children, and taught with authority, they were
unimpressed; and their involvement, if any, was
superficial.

Jesus read their hearts and anticipated their response as he told this parable. When they would come to their senses and realize that this rabbi was the Son of the living God, the long-awaited Messiah, then and only then would they argue and plead, "Don't you remember us? We listened to you in our villages. We were delighted with your humor and charmed by your stories. We were amazed at your genius and impressed with your theology. We even went to banquets in your honor and drank your homemade wine. Certainly you remember us!"

No, Jesus couldn't remember them, and he certainly wasn't impressed with their subterfuge. His inability to recognize them was not because they were only a part of the huge crowd on the Mount of Beatitudes. His inability to recognize them was not because they were indistinguishable in the crowded room at the wedding feast. The reason Jesus couldn't remember them was not because they had been lost in a crowd, but because they had never met, person to person, as Redeemer and redeemed. No matter how great the crowd, Jesus never forgets those who personally commit their lives to him.

These late arrivals were exposed for what they were: pretenders. But Jesus didn't buy their pretense. They were there when Jesus turned water into wine and they marveled at its exquisite taste. They were there when Jesus took the young maiden by the hand and interrupted her sleep of death. They were there when Jesus fed thousands with only a couple of fish and some tiny loaves. They were there when Jesus made the blind to see, the lame whole, the lepers clean. They had heard how he had calmed the sea and walked on water, and they had heard him personally when he said that the pure in heart shall see God.

These late arrivals had been intrigued, thrilled, amazed, dumbfounded, impressed. They had been bewildered, confused, frustrated, angered. They had been eyewitnesses, observers, informers—but believers they were not.

Now, as they arrived shortly after the door had been

shut and the festivities begun, they not only tried to get in, they wanted to join the party. Then, but only then, they realized what they were missing, and why. They had, however, one more recourse: persuasion. If they could talk the householder into opening the door, their worries and fears would be over. If not, they had only started.

Since the story implies that they arrived shortly after the door was closed, they could have argued that they were unavoidably detained en route. We don't know all the arguments used, but they can be easily imagined. What we do know is this: they pounded on the door, gaining the attention of the householder. He responded, not by opening the door but probably a small window in the door. Then they begged to be admitted—"Don't you remember us? We're old friends from way back. Remember when we listened to you on the streets of Nain and when we went together to the wedding in Cana?" Such pretense. The householder saw through it immediately.

Unimpressed, the householder was not swayed by their sudden sincerity, nor by their instant cordiality. They had realized their folly (a costly undertaking having an absurd or ruinous outcome), but seeing the merriment within and realizing their exclusion, they wanted desperately to get in. The householder, however, was adamant. "Look," he said, "I'm not impressed with your pretense. If you really were sincere, you'd have been here on time. All your pleading and tears will not change your status. You are pretending to be old friends of mine, but I don't know you. Actually you are my enemies, not my friends. Now get out of here!"

According to the Scriptures, there will be many surprises in the Kingdom. Many who were expected to be there will be missing, and some who were not expected will be there.

Pretense is an incredible gambling with one's soul. There are many pious, devout, basically good people— probably like some of those Jesus was addressing along with the questioner—who have never actually responded

to the invitation. Time is running out, or may have
already run out, for many of them. Foxhole conversions
do exist, we know, but they are few and far between and
are not to be counted on.

Then there are others—ostentatious, super-spiritual,
sanctimonious pretenders—who know their pretense, but
still hope that forgiveness will be more forgiving than
it can possibly be. The householder, like the host who
faced the five young maidens, could not open the door.
Time had run out. Going through the motions,
nonchalantly or recklessly or in any other way, is a
life-style not to be recommended, especially if hoping
for eternal leniency.

This complicated parable was triggered by a still
unanswered question: "Lord, will only a few be saved?"
Jesus, to some, may have implied that because the door is
narrow, only a few will be there. Getting into St. Isaac's
Cathedral in Leningrad required a pass and crowding
through a small door. Once admitted, however, we were
not only dazzled by its inner beauty but by the masses of
people within. Somewhat of an addict to my camera, I
think I lost my family three times in the crowd. But this
isn't what Jesus meant by a narrow door. He meant that
there is one entrance and only one, and whoever wants to
enter must go through that door. The size of the door had
nothing to do with the size of the crowd.

There are those who enjoy quoting statistics on eternal
affairs. At best, this is only guesswork. But one thing is
certain: those who wait until the last moment to enter, or
who make a pretense at accepting the invitation, will find
the door not only too narrow but too formidable.

A make-believe life-style of pretense is not only pure
folly, it is a miserable way to live. It is not spiritually
satisfying or rewarding, nor is it attractive to others.
For those who are looking for the householder's house,
the door is still open—but it may close at any moment.
Right now there is room for at least one more, but this will
not always be true.

Pretense, fatal to unbelievers, is a miserable existence

for Christians. To live a double life is always hazardous
and often intolerable. Even so, some seem to prefer it. It
makes one think of the grocer's family who almost never
knew what it was like to eat well. Throughout his life, the
perhaps well-intentioned but deluded grocer brought
home only the food that was unfit to sell—bruised
bananas, stale bread, and other foods difficult to market.
What a way to live!

Jesus was merciless on pretense, not only because it
kept people from getting to the door on time, but also
because it kept people from being first-rate citizens in the
Kingdom after going through the door.

CHAPTER EIGHTEEN
REALISM—
THE TOWER BUILDER
AND THE WARRING
KING
Luke 14:26-33

The two characters in this parable bit off more than they could chew—a malady common to most of us.

These two stories create one parable and reinforce the challenge Jesus had just given, with less force perhaps, but more intrigue. What Jesus had just spoken, if taken too literally and out of context, could easily be misinterpreted—or misappropriated. However, Jesus guarded against this as he told more of his ingenious stories.

In the preceding chapter we saw that certain individuals regarded Jesus indifferently until too late. Then they realized their folly. Their desperate attempts to remedy the situation proved futile. In this parable we have the opposite extreme. Certain persons, believers and unbelievers alike, took Jesus too seriously. So serious were they that Jesus was obliged to caution them that the Christian style of life can be almost unbearable at times.

To make certain they understood, he almost, it seems, painted too bleak a picture: "If any comes to me and does not hate his own father and mother and wife and children and brothers and sisters, yes, and even his own life, he cannot be my disciple."

Having said this, Jesus didn't withdraw his comment or soften it, but he did highlight it with a pair of intriguing stories which count as a single parable.

There was a certain man who owned a piece of land. Evidently he was getting tired of having his land exploited, the chickenhouse raided, and his vineyards stripped. In order to put a stop to this, he had to have some control over the land. One way would be to dig a ditch around it; another would be to plant a hedge. Both would take too long. Therefore, he decided to build a watchtower. From this observation point he could guard his entire property.

It was a reasonable decision. Without much planning or counting the eventual cost, he simply went ahead, laid the foundation, and began the tower. Before he had gone very far, he ran out of resources and had to abandon the project.

His neighbors, many of whom already had towers or hedges, realized what had happened. Before long the gossips were at it, and the hapless farmer became the laughingstock of the province.

Here we are tempted to speculate on his folly. No doubt his problem was real, his motives pure, his strategy sound. His mistake was poor judgment. Perhaps he built too elaborately (some of these towers doubled as storage bins and rest shanties). Perhaps he built too hastily, wasting needlessly. Perhaps he built too tall or big. We don't know, but it appears that Jesus intended that we give him the benefit of the doubt. He was a man whose motives were superior to his realism.

The other story is quite another tale. Here we have a king, probably a tribal head or a king of a small dominion.

Realism—The Tower Builder and the Warring King

For some reason he decided to wage war against his neighbor. For some equally strange reason, he underestimated the strength of his neighboring tribal head's army. He no sooner set out to attack than he dispatched a rider with a white flag waving mercifully against the blue sky. He surrendered without tossing a spear!

The warring king might have had legitimate grievances. He, too, might have been experiencing difficulty with his land and crops. He might have realized that his neighbor was raiding his chickenhouse and stripping his grapevines. On the other hand, he might have simply been a troublemaker, greedy for more land, power, and prestige, desiring that which didn't rightfully belong to him. Whether his grievance, if any, was enough to warrant war, we do not know, but it seems doubtful.

When word got around, he too became the brunt of many jokes. No one, his neighbors would reason, could be that stupid. So the stories were told: one with obvious positive empathy, the other with none.

It is hardly conceivable that Jesus would use two stories of near identical substance when one would suffice. Therefore, our assumption is that Jesus is telling one parable with two different stories. But why? That is the interesting problem of this parable in the light of its setting. Let us move on.

Why are certain believers willing, even anxious, to risk their lives to serve the cause of Christ? And why are certain believers unwilling or reluctant to risk anything?

In the previous chapter, the problem was one of wasting an opportunity. Some had heard the message of Jesus and listened to his clarion call to forsake everything to become his disciples. While living their normal lives, they must have been at least a little curious because even though the invitation had expired, they were curious enough to investigate. They had a chance but acted too late.

Now we have certain people who were too zealous. They were too willing to sell their farms and businesses in order to follow the new rabbi. Jesus, because of his nature, would not want to encourage people to become disciples without letting them know the possible consequences. Therefore, he told them dramatically that discipleship was serious business. In fact, it could be a matter of life or death.

Jesus was not trying to scare them off, although it may appear that way; he was firmly, even dramatically, trying to make a crowd come to its senses (crowds rarely think rationally). With this in mind, Jesus shocked them by telling them bluntly that if they wanted to be his disciples, they must renounce everything dear to them: family, friends, farms, fame, fortune. "Think it through," urged Jesus. "Plan ahead. Don't make any rash promises you cannot keep."

Both stories (the hapless farmer and the warring king) stressed the unwise strategy of failing to look far enough ahead. Evidently certain individuals were rushing headlong into Christianity without considering the cost. They had more zeal than wisdom, more integrity than intelligence, more enthusiasm than endurance.

Having said this, Jesus probably put the brakes on a wholesale stampede of the crowd. It was a matter of sobering the multitudes into becoming realistic. Whatever one thinks of Billy Graham's techniques, it is obvious that Mr. Graham, after making the altar call, simply stands before the audience, arms folded across his chest, and waits. There is no undue emotion, no pleading, no tear-stained stories. For this he should be admired. A crowd can easily be aroused into behavior it later regrets or renounces.

Becoming a Christian at that time and place wasn't exactly peaches 'n cream. In spite of the warning, Jesus not much later was powerless to stop the crowd from crowning him king; yet, how many in that emotional, excited crowd on Palm Sunday were in the angry mob which turned against Jesus days later, only God knows.

Having said what he did, we can better understand why Jesus told the story of the enthusiastic, well-meaning, but not very far-thinking landowner. The message is

Realism—The Tower Builder and the Warring King

clear: before building a tower, count the cost! Before becoming a Christian, count the cost!

However, if the warring king was a rascal (as we are inclined to think), the impact cannot be quite the same. The king was poorly although highly motivated, but his plans were totally unrealistic as well. If his motives were less than honorable, dare we suggest that the motives of some who were rushing to follow Jesus were less than noble?

Why would any want to follow Jesus without counting the cost, without a genuine interest, without an honorable motivation? The answer is perhaps the same as it is today.

Some were probably simply going along with the crowd. If everyone is following Jesus, then that's the thing to do. If Christianity is the "in" thing, then Christianity is the religion to follow. Mob psychology and peer pressure, both operative then as well as now, are often ruthless persuaders and need equally distracting dissuaders.

Others simply failed to grasp the intent of the message Jesus was proclaiming. They may have thought Christianity was an easy religion. After all, Jesus signaled the end of the legal and sacrificial systems and was ushering in an era of love, grace, and mercy. This, of course, was true, but could be badly misunderstood.

Some may have felt that they could easily keep their own religion—paganism or Judaism—and simply add Christianity to it, or those teachings which they liked the best. Jesus continually fought the notion that Christianity is an add-on religion. It was all or nothing, and Jesus made this painfully clear when he advocated despising, hating (or better understood, renouncing) everything previously held dear.

No doubt there were those who were enchanted with Jesus. Isaiah prophesied that Jesus would not be of such looks and stature that people would be attracted to him physically; but certainly—simply because of who he was and what he did—he must have possessed considerable charisma. Therefore, he felt obligated to tone it down rather than exploit it. He was not willing that any should perish, nor was he willing to coerce anyone against his or her will.

Jesus was a hometown boy who had done well ("What good thing has ever come out of Nazareth?"). Unquestionably, he must have been a folk hero, and on more than one occasion Jesus had to escape from the crowds. We know that once he was so exhausted he slept through a terrifying—to his veteran disciples—storm. This, too, was a problem the One who had put Galilee on the map had to play down.

If Jesus were considered something of a folk hero or a superstar, there would be many who would be frightfully disillusioned if they didn't realize what they were doing when aligning themselves with him. Even so, most of these were not possessed by motives of the kind suggested by the warring, foolish, blundering king.

This leads us to one more category of followers. There were those who felt that they had something to gain, politically, by following the new rabbi from Nazareth. They were disillusioned with the hierarchy in Jerusalem and had an almost fanatic hope in the sudden appearance of the Messiah who would save their necks, not their souls. Although they undoubtedly had misgivings about this Jesus, they were willing to risk their futures on him. They recognized the miraculous powers of Jesus, and saw in him a certain unexplainable charisma and leadership ability. Unless someone else quickly appeared, they were not quite willing to write him off as a potential national hero who would free them from Roman tyranny. To them, also, Jesus said, without signaling them out except in the parable, they better count the cost before jumping on his bandwagon.

Realism is an essential ingredient, both in assuming the Christian faith as well as in living the Christian life. It is one thing to be naive or simplistic; it is quite another matter to be unrealistic.

A realistic disciple of Jesus may not fully comprehend

where he is going or what will happen, but he does know
the important basics of discipleship. He knows that
Christianity is a faith for all folks, but it is not a folksy
religion.

Being realistic means assessing our lives and situations,
and then doing something reasonable about it. Being
unrealistic is foolishly fighting for our rights or desires
in an irresponsible way.

Being realistic is making our Christian life-style top
priority in our lives. Being unrealistic is going along
with the crowd, taking from the Christian faith that which
is convenient or advantageous.

The hapless farmer and the warring king were, among
other things, unrealistic. They dramatically remind us of
the importance of not overestimating our resources by
underestimating the costliness of our zeal. They also
point out the ever important but always dangerous
problem of overestimating our strength while
underestimating the power of our adversary.

CHAPTER NINETEEN
INGENUITY—
THE SHREWD
EMPLOYEE
Luke 16:1-8

A certain rich man hired an accountant to manage his
affairs. The accountant evidently had been mismanaging
the accounts, cheating the employer. Rumors began to
stir, causing the wealthy man to investigate the crooked
comptroller, resulting in the employee's dismissal.

Calling him into his office, the employer asked to see
the books. The wily accountant said he'd need time to
finalize his report (at that time financial records in the
form of handwritten IOUs were kept by the accountant).

Hastily, the crooked comptroller called in each client.
In a grand show of magnanimity, the accountant said that
business was so good that he was able to personally
reduce their indebtedness. The first debtor owed a
considerable amount of oil. He was told to cut the
indebtedness in half. Another was told to reduce his debt
of wheat by 20 percent.

One by one the debtors brought their IOUs and were told to reduce them, in their own handwriting, which was an unorthodox but legal method.

As the comptroller did this, he was shrewdly gaining their personal gratitude as he was cheating his boss. No doubt he made it clear that this was his own doing, not that of a magnanimous employer. What he was doing was obvious. Seeing the handwriting on the wall, he was protecting his future.

He knew he couldn't dig ditches, nor could he beg. Evidently there were not too many accounting positions available, and he also knew he would be blacklisted even if there were jobs open. His plan, although immoral, was ingenious.

When the employer found out what had been going on, he shrugged his shoulders, congratulated the cunning accountant for his shrewdness—and there the story ends.

It is quite easy to think that in this parable Jesus was approving the shrewd dishonesty of a desperate rascal. Nothing could be further from the truth.

No doubt the disciples wrinkled their brows, wondering what their master was trying to tell them this time. Jesus, who told this parable to his disciples, evidently had a couple of things in mind: he was preparing them for their future when he would be taken from them; he was also predicting what was to be the most stunning challenge of their entire career—a matching of wits against the wily, astute, cunning, shrewd, crafty, and yes, diabolical world they would face.

In the preceding chapter we saw how Jesus tried to get his followers to be realistic. Now we see why—from a different perspective.

Christianity has been and is engaged in a titanic struggle. It is often a matter of sheer survival, a survival of the fittest. As mentioned previously, parables must always be interpreted within the framework of all Scripture. In addition, a heavy dosage of common sense is necessary. This alone, apart from a reasonable understanding of the parable, means that Jesus was not

endorsing the dishonest behavior of the desperate
accountant. Never does Jesus approve of dishonesty or
theft, blackmail or extortion, immoral or illegal oppor-
tunism. When the rich man realized what had been done,
and the difficulties involved in undoing the damage, his
reaction was highly irregular. Most employers rarely
compliment scoundrels who cheat them.

We must remember that Jesus also created a parable in
which the injured party sent an army to vindicate his
damaged ego and to get revenge. Juxtaposed against this
parable, the attitude of the injured businessman is even
more unusual—but unusual for an important reason.

However, when we overallegorize, we run into
difficulties. To say that God is represented by the snubbed
king as well as the outwitted employer is reasonable—to a
degree—but if the real purpose of each parable is
obscured, it means that God gets revenge in one situation
and shrugs it off in another. The king mentioned above
may have been mocked, but God isn't! The well-to-do
employer may have been outwitted, but God is not!

Jesus, true to his nature, pushed the disciples as far as
he dared. He knew their road would be rocky. He knew
they would be snubbed, mocked, censored, intimidated,
falsely accused, outwitted, and even martyred. He knew
they would be lambs in a sea of wolves. He knew they
would need every ounce of wit and wisdom they could
muster.

There would be lawsuits and false witnesses, boycotts
and blacklists, blackmail and booby traps. Jesus was also
a realist. Were he to tell his disciples all they could
expect, he would break their spirit. They would have
prematurely faced danger and death with excessive
trepidation. Wisely, he withheld the details, fortifying
them with an offbeat but ingenious principle: *outwit
before you are outwitted!*

Unless the disciples were willing to be ingenious, to
outwit their enemies, to utilize every advantage possible,
the society they were to save would destroy them.

The crafty comptroller in the parable was paving the

way for his future. By building goodwill, getting his master's clients endeared and indebted to him, they would—voluntarily and otherwise—see him through the crisis of a curtailed career. He was physically (and probably mentally) unable to do physical labor, and he was too proud to beg. He had doubtless lived well, enjoying his legitimate salary plus that which he sidetracked into his own coffers. He did not care to reduce his standard of living nor change his life-style. Whether he or his employer had the last laugh we are not told!

At this juncture there are two matters for the record. Jesus is commending the accountant, not for his dishonesty but for his wisdom in thinking ahead. Christians have a tendency to take too seriously another admonition of Jesus: "don't worry about tomorrow." This of course is excellent advice, properly understood, but it does not negate the wisdom of giving thought to the game plan of one's life. The wily rascal was thinking of his future, and for that he was commended.

The other thought is this: he made friends—as many as possible—to help him secure his future. With these newly acquired friends—at varying prices—he hoped to guarantee his tomorrow. Shrewdly he used people who previously were merely impersonal IOUs in his employer's portfolio.

Jesus, in effect, is saying, "Go and do likewise." We are instructed to make as many friends as we can with people around us—in every imaginable situation. We are not to despise unbelievers simply because they are unbelievers. Cultivate their friendship, learn their ways, see what makes them tick—because we are going to need all the friends and expertise we can get. Survival is at stake.

Jesus said his disciples would be entering communities where they would be in the minority. If not careful, they would be outwitted. This is something believers cannot afford, either for their own sake or for the cause to which they are sent.

Jesus is trying to impress upon us that we cannot

impress others with a second- or third-rate life-style. If we
are extended courtesies, what happens if we fail to
reciprocate? If they throw the legal systems against us,
what happens if we do not know our rights?

Paul was a genius (another reason for his amazing
success) at using his culture to preserve his integrity. He
was not hesitant to throw his Roman citizenship around
when he needed it. He even refused to leave the
Philippian jail until the magistrates personally escorted
him to freedom. He wanted them to apologize for their
legal blunder. When it was to his advantage—or that of
his faith—he even appealed to higher, even the highest
court. Paul was no fool; he was ingenious.

Jesus in effect told his disciples not to let everyone walk
all over them, but it was more than that. He told them
to take advantage of every situation, not in a petty way,
but as an ingenious method of making Christianity
credible as well as secure.

Returning to the States after an extended absence, not
only were we chilled by some of the cinema and TV fare,
we were also warmed by some of the Christian
programming. Some of it—but not all—was high-class. If
not following certain secular formats, it was at least
influenced by them. Colorful settings, skillfully
dubbed-in sound tracks, effective talk shows, imaginative
camera work, sophisticated scripts, and highly
professional techniques were used. Gone was some, but
not all, of the amateurism of Christian programming
of the past.

This would gladden the heart of Jesus, because he
would tell his disciples today exactly what he said two
thousand years ago: second-rate amateurism is not good
enough. Learn from the experts, Jesus would advocate,
and then surpass them. In no way can Christians—a small
minority at best—pioneer every field, but we can and
must cooperate with the pioneers.

The Kingdom of God is at war—declared and
undeclared—with a wily, shrewd, manipulative general
who seems at the moment to be winning the battle.

Countless persons are defecting to his side in the ultimate showdown.

Little wonder, really. Too many Christians are ill-equipped for the battle, partly because they fail to realize that it is a battle, and partly because of a failure to understand the implications of this parable.

A godless minority has cleverly used law courts to reduce the influence of Christianity in public places; the Bible has been banned as an unnecessary piece of sectarian propaganda, obscuring its literary and humanitarian genius in the process. The state has neatly protected itself from biblical incursions by either removing itself completely from the influence of the Church or by cunningly incorporating the ecclesiastical structure into the civil body.

The impact of a Christian outrage has been effectively neutralized by several artful dodges: pornography is legitimized as an expression of freedom; prostitution is called a "redemptive catharsis"; juveniles "get away with murder" because of their "tender age"; criminals go free to flout the law and repeat offenses because of flimsy technicalities.

Christendom has also been less than ingenious in the way it has handled these artful dodges. It too has bungled many of its own internal affairs, including the mockery of defiant, rebel clerics and radical rabble-rousers (without a cause). Unwise blue laws have made a mockery of otherwise well-intentioned but naive crusaders. Mass media religious hucksters have bled a believing but sometimes gullible audience.

Jesus warned against this. He said that Christians would not only be thrown to the lions—they would also get Christian principles cleverly thrown into their faces. Many Christian virtues such as compassion, tolerance, meekness, forbearance, and love have been shrewdly used to cover a multitude of sins—blatant and otherwise. God is not mocked, but Christians sometimes are. Jesus said we must be "wise as serpents but as harmless as doves." However, he did not say that we should be either sneaky

snakes or passive pigeons. There was a method in his
madness—if we dare use this cliche again—when Jesus
commended the cunning comptroller.

Then, too, we see other less than ingenious behavior.
Some Christians unwisely use their ingenuity in dodging
responsibilities and liabilities imposed by a secular and
often antagonistic society. Church bodies at times bend
laws out of shape to avoid taxation or in circumventing
cumbersome regulations. Bogus credentials have made a
farce out of Christendom, and certain cultic bodies—
posing as Christian—have effectively soured innumerable
persons as they exploit the good name of Jesus Christ and
the Church. Should the Church stand by, expecting civil
authorities to expose this sham, or is that also the task
of the Church? In the light of the parable, it would seem
that the Christian community has an obligation to be more
ingenious than its adversaries and go on the offensive to
reduce any and all defamation where it exists. Strong
words, but so was the parable.

Jesus knew this would happen. That's why he made it
emphatic that Christians must use every ounce of
ingenuity, not only in presenting the Good News, but in
preserving its integrity. In doing this, Christians are to be
commended for maintaining an ingenious life-style in
combating the wiles of the adversary, because we wrestle
not against flesh and blood but against principalities and
powers who are ruling the world.

The shrewd employee did us a favor. He was
commended, not because he duped his employer, but
because he used his head. A life-style that encourages a
simplistic Christianity is no match against an aggressive,
wily society, sub-Christian and otherwise.

A godly ingenuity—not the illegitimate, sly, tricky type
practiced by the cunning comptroller, but an astute,
competent, proficient creativity—is not an option. It is a
mandate, not only for survival but for the integrity and
expansion of the Christian faith.

CHAPTER TWENTY
RESPONSIBILITY—
THE SERVANT
DOING HIS DUTY
Luke 17:7-10

One of the most difficult aspects of a satisfying life-style involves getting a proper perspective on responsible living. Irresponsibility is a terribly unrewarding vice, but practiced by many in spite of its demoralization.

Jesus was talking to his disciples as he spoke this parable. Evidently he was anticipating certain difficulties ahead because the story he told them—in spite of what seems to be an incongruity—most likely had a bearing on their concern raised in verse 5: "Lord, increase our faith." The disciples also must have become a bit apprehensive about the future, and in their closeness—a dozen plus one living together—Jesus no doubt sensed their uneasiness. It was in this setting that Jesus told this "dry little story about the Farmer and his Man"—as one scholar understated the parable.

People are people and need people parables, especially
in the area of these troublesome twins: the division-of-
labor and the chain-of-command phenomena. Which
disciple should serve as treasurer? Who should plan the
itinerary? When should they move on to the next village?
How should they devise their strategy? Where should
they spend their vacation?

Vacation? We must remember that Jesus more than once
wisely withdrew in order to recharge his batteries, and at
least once took a vacation on the beautiful Mediterranean
shores not far from present-day Beirut.

Was there a chain of command evident or about to
emerge among the disciples? Had they agreed on their
division of labor? Was it determined that Peter would take
charge in the absence of Jesus? Was it inevitable that
John—a creative brooder, perhaps—would drive the
others up a wall? Would Thomas, the doubter, tend to
sway them into negativistic thinking? Did Matthew,
skilled at handling monies, resent the fact that Judas
held the money bag?

It is in this light that Jesus told what appears to be a
rather dull story about a modestly successful farmer who
hired a man to work for him. This man, when hired,
agreed to both wages and responsibilities. While the
farmer had his own duties—which were not the concern
of the hired man—the hired man was expected to plow
the fields, tend the sheep, and prepare the evening meal.
Then when evening came, the farmer would be served by
the hired man who would eat later. There were no
problems. The chain of command and the division of
labor were settled.

This is why Jesus posed the rather ludicrous situation
of an employer who fixed the evening meal and told his
hired man to hurry up and sit down at the table with him.
This is just not the way it was done in that culture.

Since it had already been agreed, it was not necessary
—nor was it wise—for the farmer to thank his hired man
for simply doing his duty. He was expected to plow the
fields, tend the sheep, prepare the meals. If he thanked the

employee for everything he was hired to do, the farmer
would soon lose control and would end up begging,
pleading, and negotiating to the point of ridiculousness.
The hired man was not doing his employer a favor; he
was simply doing his duty.

This does not mean that the farmer would be boorish
or unappreciative, ignoring normal courtesies and
belittling human dignity. But it did mean that each knew
exactly what was expected, and both operated as
responsible, mature people.

Jesus then turned to his disciples, directly, saying that
this story was applicable to them. They were not lords of
the fields but laborers. They were not calling the shots;
they were obeying orders, doing their duty, accepting
responsibility. Why, then, should the disciples expect
profuse thanks or rewards for doing their duty any more
than the hired man?

Of the plausible explanations of this parable, few make
sense unless an educated guess is made in regard to that
which triggered the story. Uprooted from their daily tasks,
separated from families and familiarities for an extended
period, and engaged in a noble although vague task
(faithfully following an unknown itinerant rabbi), the
twelve must have been plagued by tensions, appre-
hension, doubt, and at times feelings of frustration—
even absurdity. No wonder they asked their master to
increase their faith!

The answer received was hardly a compliment. If they
had faith the size of a mustard seed (one of the smallest
imaginable entities), they would be able to uproot a tree,
not with their hands but with their minds. The
implication is a multiple one: a small amount of faith is
incredibly powerful . . . their faith at this stage was less
than this . . . faith has power over the physical as well as
spiritual. Whatever the real reason Jesus had in mind, he
seems to have let his answer linger but a moment on this
note and moved on.

If we may suggest that St. Luke was not putting the
words of Jesus into a random sequence (Luke was much

too skilled a writer to do that), the parable does have a direct relationship to their request for more faith.

When Jesus told them that they should not expect praise or rewards for accepting and fulfilling responsibilities, Jesus probably knew something we don't know. More than likely they had been grumbling or musing about their future. This admonition—"Do your duty without fanfare"—could sound rather chilly, even frigid, if not properly understood.

A number of years ago I visited a family in Mexico City. A stateside friend of ours was married to a Mexican physician. While conversing around a sandwich, I happened to get a glimpse of their very inconspicuous maid, a pretty Mexican teenager. Unaccustomed as I was to this luxury, I asked if she lived with them. She did. It was then our hostess voluntarily informed me that due to cultural differences, the maid would not thrive much less survive if she were treated as a family member. She had been conditioned by generations of her own people, and the only security she knew was to fulfill her responsibilities in her own way—by keeping out of sight, eating her own food, and sleeping on the floor in the kitchen. Our hostess assured us that she had offered the young girl a room of her own as well as family-member privileges but was repeatedly turned down. It would have destroyed her identity, and she couldn't have coped with it.

This is a cultural custom parallel to the situation at the time of Jesus. The disciples understood the parable perfectly even if we do not (although they might have had difficulty with its application). The message Jesus was imparting cannot be fully understood in terms of a Western culture—at least in the North. Again, we must think Palestinian. Then the rather dry ol' story will gradually become much more than that.

Verse 11 informs us that the disciples soon moved on to Jerusalem, which was the beginning of the end. Jesus knew that the disciples would soon be on their own. No longer would he be able to settle their squabbles or answer their questions. No longer would he be able to

fight their battles or silence their critics. No longer would
he be able to assign roles or suggest strategies. And no
longer would he be able to pat them on the back or give
them a friendly kick in the right direction.

When they asked for—or even demanded—more faith,
it might have been a rather genuine concern, but a little
naive. If it had been completely legitimate, Jesus probably
would have treated it differently. "All you need," Jesus
implied, "is a tiny bit of faith." A tiny bit of faith,
however, is dynamite—and the disciples were not yet
ready for such power.

Jesus, by his next remarks, must have sensed that they
were (paradoxically) getting too big for their britches.
They wanted the power Jesus had: to perform extra
special miracles . . . to confound wily wizards hell-bent
on making them look like fools . . . to turn water into
wine, walk on water, raise people from the dead, defy
mother nature. They also wanted, righteously, to smile at
those who snarled at them; but unrighteously, they
wanted special privileges and powers.

If this were not the case, Jesus would hardly seek to
put these words into the mouths of his mostly but not
always faithful twelve: "We are simple hired servants,
Lord. We do not need to be thanked for what we have
done. We have simply done our job, fulfilling our
responsibilities to the best of our ability. We are hired
men, contented with our jobs and powers. We are not
employers—why should we act as though we are?"

Just as the hired man was yet unable to assume the
responsibilities and privileges of his boss, neither were
the disciples ready to take over the role of Jesus. Not long
after this, the disciples did try.

They tried to keep little children away from Jesus and
were promptly rebuked. Later, one of the aggressive
disciples almost whacked off the head of a threatening
Roman soldier. On another occasion, some of the
disciples wanted to call fire down from heaven to cremate
certain wicked citizens.

As with all of us, the disciples had to crawl before they

could walk, which is what they were doing these three years: learning to accept, understand, delegate, and carry out responsibility. They were learning the law of the chain of command and its twin, the division of labor. Although graduation was just around the corner, they were not quite ready.

Since we are unable to eavesdrop on all the discussions which followed the telling of parables, we must do our own kind of belated eavesdropping. Could it be that the disciples wanted to be thanked for their services and faithfulness, forgetting that as ambassadors of Jesus Christ they had no responsibilities requiring rewards or awards? It appears quite likely that Jesus was prompting them to exercise their discipleship without his having to nag—or to praise them when they did.

This malady has nagged Christendom century after century: What do I get out of it? Will it increase my earnings or decrease my leisure? How will it affect my life-style? Will there be rubies or sapphires in my crown?

Years ago—and currently practiced in some circles—children (and grown-ups) were amply rewarded for attending Sunday school. As a youth, I missed one Sunday after nine-plus years of perfect attendance, failing to get the coveted ten-year award. What a blow! That was in the era when perfect attendance meant just that: *perfect* attendance.

We've come a long way since then, in some ways. Now some churches pay Sunday school teachers for teaching, and we make it worthwhile for musicians, officers, gardeners (while those with retired green thumbs wonder how and where they can serve), and we even compensate volunteers.

Certainly a person is worthy of his hire, but as this reward-award system proliferates, it can threaten the spirit of Luke 17. Of course, not all volunteerism is healthy either. Christendom constantly must strive to maintain a delicate balance between an effective volunteerism and a necessary professionalism, a matter remarkably anticipated by the master storyteller.

Responsibility—The Servant Doing His Duty

Hidden beneath the exterior of this rather inconspicuous parable lurks another formidable subject. Why was Jesus concerned lest the hired man think he were equal to the farmer? Probably because the disciples faced the same problem.

The mother of a couple of the disciples wanted Jesus—and personally asked him—to place her sons into positions of prominence (she knew not what she was asking).

Peter was doubtless the undisputed leader, but was it because he was the ex-head of a fishing fleet on leave of absence, or was it because he was of an aggressive, authoritarian temperament? His leadership, a bit shaky at first, did develop into a strong, positive role, although Paul had to straighten out his theology a time or two.

Each of the disciples was probably assigned various roles—at times, we would suspect, disagreeable to their dispositions. Judas Iscariot was treasurer of the baker's dozen, but Matthew might have been more acceptable to the group.

To think that Jesus had twelve model disciples who never quarreled, who were always considerate and magnanimous, who shouldered responsibilities without a grumble, who were never affected by the weather and always snapped back after a setback, who seldom if ever were plagued by doubts is to think erroneously. It is unrealistic to think that twelve men could tramp about the shores of Galilee and in the dust of Judea with no problems of a chain of command or division of labor.

This the disciples had to learn (sometimes the hard way): they were not above their master. This lesson is often difficult to learn. Familiarity, we are told, breeds contempt. Often it does. Even today we feel that we know the Lord so well that we can refer to Jesus and the disciples as J. C. and the boys. But familiarity can breed, if not contempt, at least a lack of respect or a failure to recognize who we are or who the person we are referring to is. Calling Presidents Jack, Dick, or Jimmy may not be as healthy as we would like to believe.

Jesus reminded the disciples, indirectly, that they were
servants, not masters; they "plowed fields they didn't
own and ate leftovers after serving the meal."

This familiarity syndrome suggests another thought.
Democracy is a marvelous invention, and it can function
extremely well. However, even the most democratic
structure (governing by the will of the people) bogs down
because of emerging, static, changing, and fading
hierarchies.

Jesus was the indisputable leader—a magnificent blend
of democrat and autocrat. It is doubtful that Jesus ruled
the twelve with an iron fist, but it is obvious that the
disciples did not create policy or determine strategy by
majority rule, nor did they vote on every decision. Every
collective body needs a leader. Someone must be in
charge; someone must be the final or ultimate authority.
Impasses do occur, deadlocks do stymie, majorities are
frustrated or intimidated by tyrannical minorities, and
compromises are often not only ineffective but paralyzing.

The employer in the parable may have sought the
opinion of the employee, but never did the hired man
refuse to go to work because he differed with the boss or
because the weather did not suit him. Care must be given
not to push the parable out of shape by making it say more
than it does—or less. Even though it is impossible to
develop a clear-cut case for either a democratic or
authoritarian form of rule among the disciples or within
the Kingdom of God, it can be safely said that Jesus was
telling the disciples that they were not autonomous. They
could not veto their leader, nor could they take his place.
The hired man probably did negotiate with the farmer,
but it was before, not after, the agreement was made.

Democratic procedures, important as they are, are not
always a foolproof Christian methodology. Although it
has been pointed out that authoritarian churches and
institutions seemingly grow faster and operate more
efficiently than other types, there is probably just as much
evidence that institutions are splintered—and shattered
—by authoritarian leaders. Democratic procedures do

safeguard institutions, but they can also be destructive.
Any institution can be paralyzed by endless debate and
meaningless compromise. Committees are important but
are no guarantee of either expertise or majority will. In
fact, the wag who suggested that a committee was
responsible for the creation of the ungainly camel might
have put more truth into his jesting than we care to admit.

Exactly what Jesus had in mind in creating this parable
is exceedingly challenging to the contemporary mind.
The tension between representative rule (equal rights
and majority priorities) and autocratic rule (favoring
obedience to authority) is never easily settled. It perhaps
can be said with a relatively high degree of fairness that
the farmer would have been a semi-authoritarian
landowner. He negotiated prior to hiring, and possibly
even argued and compromised to some extent. But after
the deal was made, there was no further haggling or
tomfoolery.

Up until that moment the buck stopped with Jesus, but
very quickly someone else would have to take over.
Perhaps Jesus was suggesting a form of authoritarian
democracy. The disciples were asked to follow Jesus; they
were not drafted or coerced. For three years they
voluntarily submitted their lives to the unknown. Until
the very end of their apprenticeship, they failed to grasp
the whole significance of what the Kingdom of God meant
or who Jesus really was. When Judas Iscariot elected to
sell out, he made a secret deal lest his colleagues become
suspicious. When he unceremoniously bowed out of
existence, he was replaced—not by a vote nor by
politicking. Two men of equal stature were nominated;
one was chosen, not by secret ballot but by a lottery.

There may have been considerable discussion, perhaps
even heated, before the nomination was made. But when
the lot was cast, the past was buried and forgotten as the
disciples pulled themselves together. How the new
leadership emerged we can only speculate, but the pattern
for the procedure had already been established.

Responsibility is not always readily accepted or even

understood. A responsible life-style is often a lifelong
struggle, but it is a glorious way to live. The willingness
to fit into a chain of command, accepting the joys and
heartaches of a division of labor, enables one to
understand and appreciate the levels of responsibility.
At times orders must be given; at other times they must
be obeyed. Responsibility is part democratic, part
autocratic.

We may never become president, but we can all do as
the late President Harry S. Truman reportedly did—
regardless of our station in life. We can hang a sign on the
wall or put a plaque on our desk: THE BUCK STOPS
HERE. Both the farmer and his hired man did this—each
in his own way. That's why they were both responsible
people.

CHAPTER TWENTY-ONE
VINDICATION—
THE CALLOUS JUDGE
Luke 18:1-8

Once, when I was at a very impressionable age, my father entered the house and exploded in rage. I had never seen him behave that way before. It frightened and intrigued me at the same time. Later I discovered the reason for his anger. Someone was trying to bilk one of his parishioners—an elderly widow—of her savings. Dad despised con artists, crooked judges, or anyone else who cheated another. In one emphatic blow, which nearly crippled the kitchen table, he declared war on this swindler. No son could have been more proud of his father than I that memorable day.

Deception and injustice have plagued the human race ever since Eve and Adam were hoodwinked and enticed into behavior they soon regretted. History is full of mischief—sophisticated and otherwise—which means that the disciples had little trouble imagining the scene Jesus created in this instance.

A certain judge had a reputation of being fearless. More than that, he was autonomous, disregarding the fear of God as well as the power of people. He did exactly what he wanted, letting the chips lie where they fell. Jesus actually seemed to be stressing that the judge was tough, refusing to be bought or sold by either the religious community or the secular crowd.

As he conducted business—hearing cases and evaluating evidence—he was pestered by a persistent widow who kept trying to get him to hear her case. The judge no doubt felt that her situation was probably inconsequential and ignored her nagging until it got under his skin. Finally he realized that his reputation as well as his disposition would suffer if he didn't do something. So he said he would hear her case and vindicate her ("I will vindicate her before she drives me crazy!").

This word "vindicate" once meant "to avenge," or "to exact satisfaction for a wrong." It now means confirming or substantiating the charge, then clearing of suspicion if the evidence warrants it. More than that, it also protects or defends against any opposition. In short, vindication is clearing an innocent person of a charge of wrongdoing; it is not revenge or retaliation.

Jesus made it rather emphatic—although easily misunderstood—that the judge had a reputation of fearing no one. He did what he felt he had to do, or wanted to do, without fearing either God or man. In all likelihood, the judge, although godless, was not unscrupulous. There are, and probably were then, judges who are ungodly (not God-fearing) but are professionally impartial and honest. Most judges at the time of Christ were known for their bribes and bias, not for their godliness and honesty.

We do not know if the widow was being denied her rights or if she was trying to cut the red tape. In all probability, she had a legitimate grievance and was persistent (and pesky) enough to hound the judge until he listened to her case. Apparently it was common at this time to cut through the interminable red tape by slipping the judge an acceptable gratuity (at times the distinction between a bribe and a legitimate business expense is nearly indistinguishable).

In those days, a widow was normally quite poor, unable to offer the judge a tempting gratuity. Therefore, this particular woman carefully selected her judge and literally hounded him into action. If she were to have any chance at all, it would be with this judge and in this manner.

Because she was brought before a judge rather than a tribunal, her case probably involved a monetary matter. Since she was a widow, it could have been a problem involving a debt or her inheritance. Because she was vindicated (cleared of any suspicion), it could be that she was being cheated, a victim of extortion, or conned by some heartless relative of her late husband. Whatever, her only recourse was a legal one, and the only way to get the judge to pay any attention to her was to pester him until he took notice. She knew she couldn't trust a bribe-taking judge; besides, not only did they favor influential people, including extortionists if necessary, but they were as likely to indict as exonerate, regardless of the evidence. She was at his mercy, and they both knew it.

If, on the other hand, Jesus was actually trying to create the imagery of a tarnished, crooked, hypocritical judge, the interpretation takes on a different hue. If this kind of a judge would allow a woman to pester him day after day, he would hardly be expected to vindicate her, even if she were innocent. This type of judge would be ruthless, unpredictable, heartless, prejudiced. Therefore, it seems most likely that Jesus did not have the typical judge in mind. Rather, he had the exception: godless but competent—a rarity but believable. He would be unmoved, either by the religious community (and its idle threats) or by the secular crowd (with its bribes and promises of reciprocity).

Jesus told the parable for a specific purpose (verse 1): to

encourage the disciples to keep on praying even when
they might feel it is hopeless. If a tough, godless judge
can be persuaded to listen to a persistent, nagging, pesky,
irritating, defenseless widow who had been wronged,
would it be reasonable to think that God would not listen
to one of his children? The disciples had probably never
thought of it this way, but that's why Jesus taught in
parables.

The widow—presumably poor and defenseless (unable
to get a lawyer to take her case)—needed to be cleared of
suspicion. More than that, she wanted to be vindicated.
To be accused of a wrongdoing when one is innocent is
not a happy experience. Indeed, it can be a shattering
experience for some, although others can shrug it off with
apparent ease.

Jesus has done us a tremendous favor in this parable by
using the imagery of an innocent woman who was
vindicated. Immediately we are able to identify and
empathize with the widow whose burden was greater
than she could bear. She needed help and turned to the
only person she knew who could possibly clear her name
and set her free. It is no accident that Jesus chose a
little-appreciated figure. Had he not singled out a specific
type of judge, the minds of the disciples would probably
have locked on the typical judge of the era: busy, hearing
cases, and vindicating those who could afford it or those
whose favor he might need someday. Because Jesus chose
a reputable judge (a godly judge with high principles
might have been actually nonexistent), it was believable
for the disciples to accept the highly irregular procedure
—a judge actually vindicating a noninfluential, non-
reciprocating damsel in distress.

This spirit of vindication (clearing of suspicion and
protecting the accused) is another marvelous character-
istic of a Christian life-style. It is something we can
do for others without a thought of reciprocity; furthermore, it is doing something for others which is difficult or
virtually impossible for them to do themselves. Paul must
often have seen its reverse in action, prompting him

to pen these words in that immortal chapter,
1 Corinthians 13:

A Christian life-style (love) does not gloat over the
misfortunes of others but rejoices when someone is
vindicated; besides, it always gives the benefit of a doubt
and never keeps a ledger on the foibles of others.
(verses 6, 7, paraphrased and amplified)

In short, we are to go to bat for others. If an unrighteous
judge, who neither feared God nor was influenced by
man, would take time to vindicate a luckless, pitiful
widow, how much more ought believers vindicate others,
believers or not.

There is much within Christendom needing to be
vindicated. When asked why a person is unimpressed
with the Christian faith, the typical answer is likely to
reflect merely a caricature of Christianity: there are too
many hypocrites; the church is a "rip-off"; missionaries
have no respect for indigenous cultures; religion is
scientifically incredible; Jesus couldn't possibly walk on
water; the Bible is merely myth and fantasy; Paul hated
women; the Decalogue was adequate for a primitive tribe
but ... Yes, the task of vindicating Christianity is endless
but not hopeless. One way is an honest attempt to phase
out misleading concepts whenever and wherever possible.

The judge could have argued that the poor widow was
obviously innocent, suggesting that people accept her for
what she was. But her name had been tarnished, her
reputation soiled, her future threatened. What she needed
was vindication, not sympathy or pity. When Christendom is maligned, distorted, caricatured, or incriminated,
it needs to be vindicated. It is too easy simply to shrug
it off, saying that Christianity will defend itself. As with
the widow, it can be innocent of ugly rumors and charges
but needs public vindication, a clearing of suspicion.

It has been wisely said that if someone throws mud,
don't try to wipe it off. Let it dry and it then will fall off
(or can be easily brushed clean). This is good, even sound
advice; but it is not always comforting to the one who is

muddied, nor are others always around to see what
happens when the mud dries. The Kingdom of God will
stand both the test of time as well as the ravages of hell
itself, but that does not mean that we have no responsibility in setting the record straight. So often first
impressions are lasting ones. Even the maligned widow—
who may well have been young and beautiful and not
necessarily elderly and inelegant—would often be
remembered by those who had heard of her tarnished
reputation but never heard (or remembered) the judge's
pronouncement of innocence. What a headline this would
make: PROMINENT JUDGE VINDICATES MALIGNED
WIDOW. However, it is really not enough merely to
recognize someone's vindication; it ought to be shouted
repeatedly from the housetops.

There are marvelous fringe benefits that accompany a
life-style which practices vindication. The joy one
receives when setting someone free is often difficult to
express: a pastor maligned by a miffed member; a parent
misrepresented by a punished child; a child indicted by
an irate parent; a coach scorned by an undisciplined
superstar; an artist castigated by an unreasonable critic;
a teacher blacklisted by an unscrupulous principal; an
employee fired by a rumor-believing employer; a spouse
wrongly accused by a jealous mate. To say that this is
none of our business would be to say that the widow's
grievance was of no concern to the judge. Vindication
sometimes is both messy and time-consuming. Mistakes
can be made; a foolish zeal can do more damage than
good.

Even so, the judge probably had no idea if the pesky
widow were innocent or not. Therefore, he had to set
aside other cases (possibly of a much more serious
nature), hear her story, weigh the evidence, and then
clear her before her society. It wasn't enough to listen to
her side and make a judgment; he had to gather all the
evidence and judge accordingly. He became involved—
possibly much more than he had desired—and only
vindicated her when the case was closed.

Vindication—The Callous Judge

When the woman caught in the actual act of committing adultery was brought to Jesus, no one seemingly was concerned about the woman. They had set a trap for Jesus. Remarkably, Jesus vindicated both himself and the guilty woman, admonishing her to cease her adulterous ways. Jesus also vindicated the little children who were sent away by his overprotective and nonunderstanding (although perhaps well-intentioned) disciples. Not only did he rebuke his disciples, he dramatized his love and concern for children by taking them into his arms.

Just as there is joy in heaven when someone repents, there must also be rejoicing when someone tainted or even stained by rumor or blackmail is cleared of suspicion by someone who cares.

A life-style which refuses to let the innocent suffer is one of the most noble virtues known to humankind.

To vindicate or not to vindicate—that is the question.

CHAPTER TWENTY-TWO
SELF-ESTEEM—
THE PHARISEE AND
THE TAX-COLLECTOR
Luke 18:9-14

This parable ought to be easier to understand because
Jesus told us exactly why it was spoken and to whom. It
was told to a certain select group of self-righteous
characters who, in addition to their smug religious
security, possessed another wretched life-style: they were
holier than everybody (they thought).

If it is true that everyone loves a bit of humility, it is
equally true that everyone despises a touch of arrogance.
However, we get the feeling that Jesus was not talking
to a few who were merely tainted; they were saturated
with contempt.

Furthermore, Jesus made it plain that they called their
own shots. In no way could they simply be misguided
disciples of either Moses or Jesus. They trusted in their
own ingenuity, their own interpretations, their own

life-style. So self-righteous were they, so comfortably smug, so secure, they felt they could afford to despise all others who maintained a differing style of life.

In order to cut through this arrogance, Jesus was forced to employ a powerful, penetrating parable. By actually naming one of the participants a Pharisee, Jesus intentionally divulged the objects of his attack. These men, whose cultic nuances revealed a religious body which had had much more noble aspirations in its earlier day, were not fully aware (if at all) of the depth to which they had sunk.

One of their colleagues—the principal in the parable— had gone to the Temple to pray, probably at the mid-afternoon hour of prayer. Standing in a conspicuous place, he prayed—or as some say, bragged. Actually, except for his ugly attitude, he probably was a fairly decent person. He was not an extortionist, nor did he engage in an adulterous pastime. He was just in all his dealings (although we may tend to question his honesty) and devout beyond the call of duty. Twice a week he fasted—once a year was all that was required—and as he fasted, he undoubtedly prayed for those with obvious spiritual needs. He tithed on all that he received, which probably meant that he tithed on items of inconsequential worth as well as items on which tithes had already been paid. This, too, was beyond the requirement.

More than this, he shifted his eyes in the direction of the sinful tax-collector, breathed a self-righteous sigh of relief, and told whoever was listening that he, the Pharisee, was not like this wretched man, an outcast even among his own kin.

The listening Pharisees knew Jesus was talking about them, but were powerless at the moment to do anything about it. He did get their attention, however, which was part of his strategy.

If they squirmed in self-righteous indignation at his description of them, there was some appeasement in the portrayal of the despised tax-collector. This man was on the opposite end of their self-righteous totem pole.

The typical tax-collector at that time worked beneath an alien flag, collecting taxes for a foreign power. He was known not only as a traitor but as an extortioner, blackmailing and cheating his own people. This disgusting behavior constituted the worst imaginable life-style as far as the Pharisees and the people were concerned.

Consequently, Jesus was actually taking the life-style of the culture—the continuum of best-to-worst—and pitting it against itself. The inevitable result was not what his audience wanted to hear. The self-righteous were confident that their man in the white trunks (the Pharisee) would win, but he was knocked out of the ring by the man in the black trunks (the publican).

Jesus was not giving a direct lesson on prayer nor was he condemning Pharisees or publicans per se, although he was coming down hard on Phariseeism and publicanism (which actually was synonymous with extortion). What Jesus was attempting to do in the parable was to dramatize the fact that there is no such thing as a do-it-yourself righteousness. No person, no matter how good one is, how religious one's life-style may be, or even if one goes beyond the call of duty, can earn righteousness.

Even the best (or those who assumed they were) were not good enough, and there was no way the worst could possibly justify themselves or make adequate restitution. The only way to become righteous was to follow the prayer of the penitent: "God, be merciful to me a sinner." This confession and plea, taken from the fifty-first Psalm, makes it indelibly clear that the only life-style acceptable to God is a "broken spirit and a contrite heart."

There is no other way, said Jesus in the parable. The humbled, broken in spirit with a contrite heart will not be despised. The arrogant prayer will fall on deaf ears.

Although the general understanding of this parable may not exactly suggest a definite Christian life-style characteristic per se, there is a message here which should not be overlooked.

If it were possible to extricate the most negative

characteristics from each of the two personalities mentioned in this parable, we would discover an interesting, more balanced, composite life-style. The Pharisee knew that unrighteousness as exemplified by the publican was unbecoming and wanted no part of it. In fact, he was deeply grateful, even if hypocritical, that he had been spared the repugnance of a ruthless collector of taxes.

There are some life-styles that are repugnant. The publican's cry of mercy was heard, but his reputation could haunt him the rest of his life even though his criminal tactics ceased and his sins were forgiven. In other words, certain life-styles are difficult to live down.

Both of these men teach us this. A genuinely converted but previously arrogant Pharisee would also have a struggle erasing his past reputation and establishing a believable life-style. Many, in fact, found it impossible or refused to accept the Apostle Paul's conversion because of what he had been; and Peter, when under pressure, temporarily relapsed into his old life-style—perhaps more than once. God can, and does, change hearts and life-styles, but the past can be extremely difficult to overcome. Those who advocate living boldly and even recklessly because God's grace is more than adequate to cover any sin are not doing us a favor. God forgives and forgets, but people often do not.

In getting at the heart of the prayers offered, we also find a striking thought. The prayer prayed by the broken publican was a terse, direct, imploring prayer. It was a beautiful prayer, but it should be prayed only once. To emulate this prayer and repeat it often would be to err.

A Christian life-style which constantly begs for forgiveness and mercy usually results in despondency— or worse. God's forgiveness is permanent. We need not continually rehash our transgressions, nor should we feel that we are nothing but a wretched worm. This is not so! A sinner saved by grace doesn't need to keep hanging his head in shame. He can walk with a quickened pace and with head held high; to shuffle along because we know that we have sinned and fallen short of the glory of God is not the life-style suggested by this parable.

The Pharisee, in spite of his conceit and smug self-righteousness, does us a favor by boldly going to the place of prayer, standing with head held high, and telling the world that he is happy he was spared a life of debauchery. He had problems, but lack of self-esteem was not one of them. There is reason to rejoice in being spared from living a life of extortion and adultery (plus a host of other greater and lesser debilitating maladies which plague humankind). The Pharisee's motives are suspect, but his posture is worth noticing.

The Pharisee also was a pacesetter. Although he seems to be bragging about his exploits, which is reprehensible, the competition was keen. St. Paul wasn't always a saint although he was, by his own admission, a "Pharisee of the Pharisees." That was quite an achievement! Jesus was building into this parable a character who was indeed a Pharisee of the Pharisees. Perhaps, until Paul, there was no equal. Though Phariseeism was and is an undesirable trait, the Pharisee's problem was self-righteousness and arrogance, not self-depreciation.

The Pharisee, a model in self-esteem, was thankful that he had been spared certain ills in life, but he was also able to give God at least some of the glory for these accomplishments. Self-esteem includes giving credit where credit is due as well as a willingness to take blame. The Pharisee was not content with being just another, ordinary Pharisee. Other Pharisees tithed on a net income; he tithed on the gross. They fasted occasionally; he fasted twice a week. They said their prayers at home; he went to the Temple.

What a fantastic person he would have been if he could have rid himself of his arrogance and self-righteous hypocrisy! What a Christian he might have been had he prayed the same prayer the publican prayed!

The way to a healthy life-style of self-esteem is similar to walking a tightrope. It can be done, but it takes practice —and desire. It involves trial and error, stumbling and falling, getting up and trying and trying again. And again.

In this parable we see two men stumbling through life —one of them self-confident, sure of himself, poised; the other quite the opposite. Yet the one least expected to succeed did. Why? He was exalted (raised to a higher status) because he had humbled himself. The other was unmovable, unyielding, unteachable, and even worse, unforgivable.

There is a difference between self-esteem and a godly self-esteem. The world is full of poised, charming, well-mannered, and beautifully groomed people— outwardly. Many are fooled by this good-looking facade. In contrast many, to the ordinary observer, are clumsy, self-depreciating, timid, awkward, not with it. But they have prayed the penitent's prayer; they have humbled themselves; their sins are forgiven. Their names are recorded in heaven, but they go through life beating their breasts, hanging their head, sorry for their past and unsure of the future.

This parable indicts such behavior. How did the publican get to a position of such low self-esteem? How did the Pharisee get so much self-confidence? Of course we do not know. Nor do we know how and why people act the way they do, in spite of new theories of behavior coming forth with sometimes monotonous regularity.

What we do know, however, is often overlooked. Jesus put this parable to rest with the most provocative statement: "Everyone who exalts himself will be humbled, but he who humbles himself will be exalted." In other words, we exalt or humble ourselves; it is not done for us.

Humility, like arrogance, is a do-it-yourself character-istic. Ironically, we often tend to work out the kinks in our everyday life in our own way, but seem to feel that divine intervention is necessary in order to live humbly. We see this in the semi-humorous prayer of the churchman who prayed regularly for his pastor, "Lord, we'll keep him poor; you keep him humble." Poverty no more keeps a person humble than wealth makes a person arrogant, even though there may be more conceited rich than cocky poor.

Was the Pharisee arrogant because he was well-to-do, influential, clean-cut, and religious? Hardly. He was arrogant because he worked at it. Was the publican humble because he was non-influential, irreligious, not affluent? Hardly. He probably was at least as well-to-do and influential (in his own way) as the Pharisee.

Had the publican been humbled by something traumatic in his life? That we do not know. All we know is what Jesus said: "He who humbles himself will be exalted." Therefore, the publican must have humbled himself, although it is possible he had some help along the way. Saul raised havoc among the early Christians and nearly singlehandedly extinguished the flickering flame of Christianity until he was knocked off his horse (high horse?) and blinded. But did this humble him? It brought him to his senses as he realized that the one he was persecuting was indeed the Son of the God he thought he was doing a favor. In spite of this trauma, it is doubtful that Paul was ever afflicted with too much humility, although self-esteem and self-confidence were always his lot.

Therefore, there seems to be a paradox here. No matter what it was that drove the publican to beg for mercy—unashamedly, openly, publicly, with the haughty Pharisee standing by looking on—we do know that he humbled himself. No one forced him to go to the Temple, to confess openly; no one threatened him if he didn't confess; no one blackmailed him into praying the prayer that transformed his life, giving him not only the potential of self-esteem but a godly serenity. He came on his own, voluntarily. He humbled himself even though it meant public embarrassment, possibly humiliation—although only temporarily.

But why? Had he seen the plight of widows victimized by extortion? Had he seen enough of the inglorious tyranny exercised by the Romans over his people? Had he heard the message of Jesus which pricked his sleeping conscience? Had the ancient Decalogue finally gotten to him—"You shall not steal" (extort); "You shall not [allow] murder"; "You shall not covet"; "You shall have no other gods before the true and living God"? Whatever it was, something got to him.

Jesus never did complete the story. We do not know if the arrogant Pharisee ever came to his senses. Nor do we know whether the pathetic publican ever quit beating himself.

Do we dare—for the sake of illustration—pen a sequel to the parable by suggesting that the publican, overwhelmed by the love of God, threw his shoulders back and strode over to the Pharisee in order to tell him how great it was to be forgiven? Would the Pharisee, in response, throw his arms around the publican and say, "I don't know what happened to you, but whatever it is, I want it too"?

What a scenario! It may have never happened, but that does not mean that it could not. When the love of God and the redemption of Jesus work on a person, arrogance and shame, contempt and guilt fade away. In their place emerges a new life-style of forgiveness and inner peace which leads—sooner or later (hopefully sooner)—to a life of maturity and a godly self-esteem (which is totally different from a godless self-esteem).

No wonder the publican went home rejoicing—not only because he gained (or regained) his self-respect, but because his sins were forgiven. Without this, there can be only a limited self-respect and self-esteem.

EPILOGUE

We have come to the end of a story, not because there is
no more to say but because there is a positive correlation
between indulgence and endurance.

Immediately, however, the pesky question arises,
What about the rest of the parables? Yes, there are other
very fine parables; important as they are, the line had
to be drawn somewhere. Besides, there are many excellent
volumes on the parables which can and ought to be
consulted.

Personally, it is hoped that you will continue exploring
the fascinating parables of Jesus. In no way have we
exhausted them, nor have we attempted to do that.
Hopefully we have made them readable, and possibly
opened some new vistas for you. Not everyone will agree
with all my interpretations, which is understandable—

and reasonable. While an attempt was made to explore the parables in-depth without appearing pedantic, the style deliberately employed a liberal sprinkling of cliches in order to create a certain familiarity—especially for those unaccustomed to this kind of subject matter.

St. John seemingly felt a frustration similar to mine as he finished his monumental work: "I suppose that if all the other events in Jesus' life were written, the whole world could hardly contain the books" (John 21:25, *The Living Bible*).

If your appetite for the incredible parables of Jesus has been whetted, this writer and his publisher will be gratified.

BIBLIOGRAPHY

The following bibliography is not intended to be
complete, nor is it a representative or recommended list.
It is given basically to show the reader the rather
extensive writing on the parables during the past century,
as well as the diversity both in subject matter and
authorship. Furthermore, the writer has not necessarily
drawn from these sources nor has he limited himself to
these, or other, volumes on the parables of Jesus. In fact,
some of the best insights into an understanding of the
parables do not come from books written specifically
about the parables. Therefore, the serious scholar should
keep an eye and ear open to any and all primary and
secondary sources. I hope these books will be merely a
suggestive, not an exhaustive, bibliography. You may not
be able to locate some of these books. Don't forget that

in every good, scholarly work, references to books and scholars are included, except in this study where a deliberate attempt has been made to refrain from name dropping and cluttering the pages with excessive footnotes.

Ayer, William Ward. *Christ's Parables Today* (1949). A compact series of sermons penned by an evangelist, with titles such as "Christ's Pessimism Concerning the Present Age," "Christ's Optimism Concerning the Present Age," "Are You the Prodigal's Brother?" and "Wages and Hours."

Carlston, Charles A. *The Parables of the Triple Tradition* (1975), Fortress Press, Philadelphia, Pa. This volume wrestles specifically with the synoptic problem and the parables.

Dodd, C. H. *Parables of the Kingdom* (1935; revised edition 1961), Charles Scribner's Sons, New York. Dodd, known for his "realized eschatology," sought critically for the meanings of the parables in their original historical setting.

Drysdale, F. B. *Holiness in the Parables* (1952). A reminder not to overlook the moral and spiritual messages contained in the parables (in contrast to literary and critical interpretations and pictorial illustrations). The same idea is found in William Arnot, *The Parables of Our Lord* (1872); George A. Buttrick, *The Parables of Jesus* (1973), Baker, Grand Rapids, Mich.; G. Campbell Morgan, *The Parables of the Kingdom* (1960).

Hargreaves, John. *A Guide to the Parables* (1968). Allenson, Naperville, Ill. With a positive Foreword by C. H. Dodd, the paperback edition (1975, Judson Press, Valley Forge, Pa.) will be useful as a study guide. Twelve selected parables with an introductory chapter.

Hunter, Archibald M. *Interpreting the Parables* (1976) and *The Parables Then and Now* (1972), both by Westminster, Philadelphia, Pa. The latter, which stresses the practical, existential "now," is a sequel to the former (originally published in 1960) which stressed the "then." Hunter tries to bridge the gap left by scholars who tended to put the parables into a Jewish (Palestinian) straitjacket but failed to see the relevance of Jesus' words for today. He is helpful in understanding the evolution of parabolic thought down the theological roadway of 2,000 years, but particularly the past century.

Jeremias, Joachim. *The Parables of Jesus* (revised edition 1971) and *Rediscovering the Parables* (1966), both by Charles Scribner's Sons, New York. The latter is a revision of the former (originally published in 1963), omitting the greatest part of the bulk of important but highly technical and linguistic material. A most valuable treatment of the parables of Jesus and the Palestine milieu, considered by many a landmark in theological scholarship.

Jones, G. V. *Art and Truth of the Parables* (1964). This book contains a survey of the history of the interpretation of parables in addition to

Bibliography

arguing that the parables are a great form of art. This same theme is found in G. H. Lang's *Pictures and Parables* (1955) and *The Parables* (1974, Fortress Press, Philadelphia, Pa.) by Dan O. Via.

Lockyer, Herbert. *All the Parables of the Bible* (1963), Zondervan, Grand Rapids, Mich. In its sixteenth printing (1975) with some 30,000 copies in print, this ambitious volume does a lot of digging in both Testaments for any and all parables. Lockyer discovers and analyzes over 250 different biblical parables. For $7.95 there is a lot of information squeezed into 371 pages, plus bibliography and indexes.

Smith, Charles W. *The Jesus of the Parables* (1975), United Church Press, Philadelphia, Pa. A temptation to place Jesus autobiographically into too many of the parables is ever present. Smith may be one of the forerunners of this trend but has many valuable points to make.

Thielicke, Helmut. *The Waiting Father* (1975), Harper & Row, New York. Sixteen chapters (fifteen parables) by the popular German preacher, professor, theologian. The original German title, *God's Picturebook*, is a provocative title for these meditations, and "The Waiting Father" is superior to, perhaps, but not as familiar as "The Prodigal Son."